WHEN PAREN

When Parents SPLIT

Support, information and encouragement for teenagers

GLYNIS GOOD

BLACKHALL PUBLISHING

Published in 2008 by
BLACKHALL PUBLISHING LTD • DUBLIN • IRELAND

© Glynis Good, 2008
© James Benn, 2008

ISBN: 978 1 84218 160 7

BA catalogue record for this book is available from the British Library.
All rights reserved. No part of this publication may be reproduced, stored in a retrieval system or transmitted in any form or by any means, electronic, mechanical, photocopying, recording or otherwise, without the prior, written permission of the publisher.

This book is sold subject to the condition that it shall not, by way of trade or otherwise, be lent, resold, hired out, or otherwise circulated without the publisher's prior consent in any form of binding or cover other than that in which it is published and without a similar condition, including this condition, being imposed on the subsequent purchaser.

This book is typeset by Ashfield Press in 11.5 on 14 point Quadraat
Illustrations by JAMES BENN
Designed by SUSAN WAINE
Printed by ATHENAEUM PRESS LTD.

ACKNOWLEDGEMENTS

The idea and seed of this book was planted by conversations with many young people looking for information and support in dealing with family separation and not always being able to find it. Without them, and their openness and willingness to share their stories with me, this book would not exist.

There are many other people who have directly or indirectly contributed to this book happening and some of these I would especially like to acknowledge:

A circle of friends (Margaret, Lindsey, Jenny and Jane) who got tired of me talking about wanting the book to exist and challenged me to stop talking and get on and write it.

Anna Chisnall for her total belief and commitment to the book and her guiding hand along its path.

James Benn, a student friend, who dropped into our home at the right time for me to hear he was studying Art and Graphic Design in college. This led us on an enjoyable and creative journey as James illustrated the book and the cover. James, you are inspirational to work alongside and thank you. (see <http://www.jbenn.co.uk>).

My colleagues in Marriage and Relationship Counselling Service (MRCS), particularly within the Teen Between® programme, for their insight, wisdom and encouragement. Special thanks to Jacinta and Lisa for reading manuscripts and offering thoughts and ideas along the way, and to the late Doreen Condon who coordinated the Teen Between® programme in Ireland with such positive enthusiasm for so many years.

All in the Living Life Counselling Centre in Bray, Co. Wicklow, who provide a great counselling service in my local area.

Jennifer O'Brien for advice and information in regard to the legal process of family separation in Ireland.

Debbie – thank you for your time, your friendship and for your red highlighting pen that directed me back on track regularly. I look forward to working together on new ideas and manuscripts in the days ahead.

Elizabeth Brennan and all in Blackhall Publishing for the privilege of working together with them. Thank you, Elizabeth, for your sensitivity to the subject and for your flexibility. Thank you to Blackhall Publishing for recognising and meeting a need to cover social issues in an Irish context.

Family is important to everyone and I am part of a huge crowd when it comes to extended family. You are definitely too many to mention individually but each one of you is important to me.

The final but most important word of appreciation is for my husband Bas, our children Heidi, Mark, Daniel and Kyle, and Omar (who has put me in the 'mother-in-law' category). You believed in me more than I believed in myself. Thank you for your enthusiasm, humour, support and love. I thank God for the privilege of sharing life with each one of you.

CONTENTS

INTRODUCTION: What Is this Book and Who Is it For?   ix

1. Finding Out   1
2. Coping at School   15
3. Stuck in the Middle   25
4. Dealing with Your Anger   35
5. Understanding Your Parents' Distress   49
6. Be Yourself   57
7. New Partners and New Babies   67
8. Families Joining Together   75
9. Special Occasions   85
10. Difficult Situations   93
11. Advice from Teenagers …   102
12. Last Word   109

APPENDIX 1:   Legal Terms   111
APPENDIX 2:   Useful Contact Information   119

WHAT IS THIS BOOK AND WHO IS IT FOR?

This is the first book to be published in Ireland to help teenagers cope with the consequences of family separation. It aims to provide support and information in helping them to address their parents' separation. It emerges from many years of working with teenagers as a counsellor and with the recognition that, beyond the small number of young people who are able to avail of counselling, there are many more who are managing family life after separation without such support.

FOR TEENAGERS

If you are a young person living in a separated family then this book is for you. Your parents may have separated a number of years ago or just recently. Every child and teenager in a family is impacted by their parents' separation and it is a painful and difficult time for everyone involved. Your parents have separated because things have gone wrong for them in their relationship. It is not your fault and you can never be to blame for this happening.

You may feel quite alone in the experience of your parents separating, but it is an experience shared by many. Statistics show that, last year in Ireland, over one hundred families separated *every week*. This represents a lot of children finding out that their parents are separating. Marriage breakdown is increasing fast in Ireland and the number of children who, like you, are dealing with their family changing is also growing continually.

You might be staying silent about what is happening at home and feel that there is nowhere or no one 'neutral' to go to for help. This book is for you to pick up and find information, support and encouragement in coping with your parents' separation. Most chapters include quotes from teenagers,* living in Ireland today, that relate their real-life experiences of their parents' relationships breaking down.

Parents are not perfect (even when they are together) and life does not always go the way you might hope. While you may feel that it is not possible to change what is happening around you, I hope this book will give you courage to make positive choices with positive outcomes to help you manage your own situation. You can also give this book to your parents to help them understand some of what is going on for you at the moment too.

FOR PARENTS

The teenage years are a time of growing, changing and moving from parental control to a greater sense of self control. This is a time when security at home should provide a foundation for moving through adolescence and all the changes required to progress safely into the adult world. Family breakdown occurring at this stage can be very traumatic. As everyone adjusts to the new situation, teenagers (caught between childhood and adulthood) feel confused as to what is expected of them in the process. Teenagers value privacy and, rather than talking or revealing the difficulties they are experiencing, will often hide their feelings and try to cope alone.

In my work I have met many teenagers who experienced family separation while they were quite young, but it was as they got older that

---

* All names have been changed to protect their privacy and identities.

they began asking questions about the separation. The teenage years can be a time of questioning, re-evaluating and making personal choices. It is a time for young people to learn how to negotiate and compromise in a more adult manner in the matters affecting them. This can be difficult. For example, how does a young person convey to a parent (whose contact time clashes with a friend's party) that his or her wish to go to the party is not a rejection of time with the parent?

This book is primarily for teenagers (within a family context), but my hope is that, as a parent, it may bring you new understanding of what your young person is coping with. Keep listening to them – they are worth listening to.

FOR TEACHERS AND GUIDANCE COUNSELLORS

Teachers may become aware that a student's ability to manage school and work has changed. Lack of concentration, lack of focus, and a change in behaviour towards teachers, his or her own schoolwork and other pupils can often be a sign that a student has something else on his or her mind.

This book will help give some insight into the complexities of a teenager's life during and after his or her parents' separation.

Finding Out

'My parents were always fighting and shouting and then they wouldn't talk to each other for days. It was just normal in our house. Afterwards, I wasn't really surprised that they separated but I still don't think I was prepared for it. I don't think anyone ever really is.' SARAH (17)

'I always thought my parents were happy and got on. We never saw anything that would have hinted that they weren't. I never saw it coming. I still can't believe that they have separated. I had no idea. It was like one day we were a happy family and the next day they were telling us we weren't. I never thought it would happen to my parents.' MARK (12)

'Separation is not something that just affects teenagers in a family but actually involves them.' JANE (18)

'No matter how much you think about your parents separating you can't actually change it or control it.' JACK (17)

'I never worried about anything really before. Now I worry about the bills and money issues.' PETER (14)

I thought my parents would be together for always.' SUSAN (13)

'Even though they did not get on very well at times and even though they argued a lot, I never thought that they would break up. I was really shocked.' ELAINE (16)

'Family separation is real-life drama and can affect anyone ... even me. You see separating families on TV and it seems upsetting but not too bad. But when it happens to you it is such a shock and is a real-life disaster.' DEE (15)

It's a fact of life in Ireland today that, every week, many people hear that their parents are separating. Your parents' relationship breaking down is a traumatic process and, if your family is going through this now, you already know that it is a deeply distressing experience for everyone. This may be a confusing time when you find yourself caught between being a child in the family (under the age of 18) and yet, as a teenager, trying to relate to the situation and everyone around you with a more mature attitude.

However difficult and upsetting things are at the moment, they will, in time, get better. Separation is not just a single event. It is a process that continues over a long time.

Process: a series of events producing change.

Life may be difficult and confusing now and you might feel as though your world has been turned upside down, but things will improve. It is important to remember that your parents' separation is about *their* relationship.

The decision to separate is seldom reached quickly by parents and will not have been easy to make. Sometimes the decision to end the relationship is made by one parent, rather than both. One parent may feel anger and resentment towards the other. It is difficult to witness this when, in the past, there used to be love and respect between your parents. Both parents will, however, be struggling with the consequences and anxieties that the separation brings.

The fact that your parents are separating does not mean that you have to stop having a good relationship with each of them individually. One thing that does not change is that they are still, and always will be, your parents.

> *Remember that your parents' separation is not your fault. There is nothing you have done to cause the separation and there is nothing you can do to change it.*

FAMILY

'At the start it can feel like your life has shattered.' AISLING (16)

Lightning is described as a high-voltage electrical discharge. Hearing that your parents are separating can leave you feeling as though you have been hit by a flash of lightning. Some of you may have been living in a stormy family and were expecting the lightning. You may even be relieved now that it has happened. For others the news has struck without any warning. Shock is part of the experience of hearing that your parents are separating. Everyone is able to remember when, where and how they found out.

Shock: a sudden impact. An experience that can leave someone feeling paralysed in the situation.

Shock:
- Is normal.
- Is not a permanent state.
- Will pass.
- Makes it difficult to think clearly.
- Confuses things.

'I just felt sick when they told us. Mum was crying. Dad was so uncomfortable. They were talking to us but I got such a shock that I didn't hear anything after they said they were separating. I just sat there and I couldn't take it in. I didn't want to hear what they were saying. I remember that day and the time like it just happened, but it is five years ago now.' EMILY (17)

'No one said anything to me. Everyone kept being odd. There were all these phone calls and crying and silences. When I asked what was going on I just got told, 'Nothing's the matter.' Yeah right! I had worked it out for myself before anyone told me. It would have been better if someone had told me. I think I deserved that much.' DON (13)

'I got a text message in school telling me they were separating – they thought it would be best for me to know before I got home from school and saw that Dad had moved out. I could hardly breathe when I read it in school. I was so angry they were separating, but I think I was angrier about getting the text.' SAM (14)

'They told us that it would be better for everyone if they separated, but this was just what suited them. They decided for us. We didn't get asked.'
BROTHERS (12 AND 14)

'My parents told me that they had been thinking of separating for years. I can't believe that I just hadn't noticed it was that bad. It came as a huge shock to me.'
DAN (15)

'My parents used to just treat each other terribly. I think it was better that they separated because we didn't have to live with them in the same house being so horrible to each other. It was quieter and not normal for a while, but better.'

MICHAEL (18)

PARENTS SUFFER SHOCK TOO

Parents will usually be in shock and struggling to deal with all their own emotions when they are talking to you. Most parents say that telling their children that they are separating is the most difficult and unwanted conversation they will ever have with them. It may be a great disappointment to your parents that their relationship is ending. Separation was not part of your parents' original plan. They never started a life together thinking that it would end.

Understandably, you want clear information now as to what is happening and what plans are being made. However, these answers are not always available because your parents themselves are unsure of how the changes will be worked out. They may need more time to sort out the practicalities.

THE AFTERMATH OF SHOCK

When you start to recover from the shock of finding out about the separation, you will experience a whole mixture of emotions. You might want to vaporise the next person who asks, 'How are you feeling?' But the fact is that feelings are experienced by us all.

> *Feelings get talked about by some, ignored by others but experienced by us all.*

The word 'sad' is often used to describe a range of emotions, such as feeling broken-hearted, depressed, disappointed, discouraged, disillusioned, downhearted, gloomy, glum, miserable or upset. That's a lot of emotion wrapped up in one small three-letter word. Writing out a list like this is not intended to make you feel more miserable. Instead it is to let you know that these feelings are normal and are what most people experience during and after parental separation.

> *When your parents separate, it is highly unlikely that you can just get up and get on with your life as though nothing very much has happened. So give yourself a chance.*

EXERCISE
Perhaps one of these characters below, or more likely a number of them at the same time, expresses your mood and feelings at this moment. You might even put a tick next to them all at some point, because sometimes when everything starts to change 'confusion rules'. Everything has changed and situations seem strange and new. You may long for the past when life was more predictable.

☐ **ANGRY**   ☐ **SAD**   ☐ **WORRIED**

☐ HAPPY   ☐ SCARED   ☐ LONELY

SO, WHAT ARE YOU MEANT TO DO WITH ALL THESE EMOTIONS THAT ARE FILLING YOUR HEAD?

> *Don't pretend that everything is OK when it isn't.*

Bottling things up won't help you in the long run. If you shake a two-litre coke bottle continuously and suddenly open it, you will leave quite a mess over yourself and whoever else is around. Pushing your feelings down just does not work because at some point you will be ready to explode.

> *Being silent makes some parents mistakenly think that you are coping and are OK, when you are not. Talking about things to someone you trust will help you cope with all your emotions – especially if you are feeling very angry or deeply sad.*

In the middle of all the upset and confusion it is really important to have someone you can talk to about how you are feeling. Your parents are the best people to talk to, but sometimes it may be easier to talk to a friend, grandparent, relation, youth worker, teacher or school counsellor.

Think about who you will talk to and put his or her name in here as a reminder:

....

> Don't bottle things up.

LIFE CAN BE TOUGH

Going through a painful emotional time is not something anyone would choose for themselves. Neither is it an experience that parents want for their children. In life, however, none of us can be protected from experiencing pain at times.

At the moment it might be the pain of:

- Not talking to a parent (whom perhaps you blame for the separation).
- Losing contact with a parent.
- Having to move house.
- Seeing your parents, brothers and sisters unhappy.

You need to remember that you are not the problem. The situation has created some of the problems you will have to deal with, but you will get through these difficult and challenging days.

Your parents' separation should not stop you from:

- Having a good relationship with both of them (in most circumstances).
- Getting on in school.
- Planning the future and what you want to study or work at.
- Having good, strong relationships in your own life.

A PERSONAL CHALLENGE

> *Your challenge is:*
> *to find a way through your family changes that involves you making good choices for yourself.*

Any choice we make has positive and negative consequences. Learning to stop and think about these before acting will take practice. You may think that you have no control over a lot of circumstances, but in fact you do have control over yourself and how you respond to the situations you find yourself in.

AMY'S STORY

'I just withdrew from everyone and kept myself in my room. In the end I realised that I was just making myself more miserable than I already was.' AMY (14)

Amy tried to deal with all that was going on after her parents' separation by avoiding everyone. She felt that her family was not normal anymore and so she told no one. Amy realised after some time that her decision to keep away from everyone was not a good choice as it was making her more miserable. When she trusted one of her friends and talked to her about everything it was a relief. This was the start of Amy taking control in a more positive way. While the situation at home did not change, Amy learned to deal with it better.

Telling no one is not a good choice. There can be a lot to deal with and having the support of even one person who will listen to you will make a difference. Knowing you can 'think out loud' with this person is important. You might say that you are not necessarily looking for his or her advice, but rather his or her support and back-up as a friend.

KEEP IN CONTACT

Do try and keep in as much contact as possible with your parent after he or she has moved out. This is not about taking sides or being disloyal to one parent. It is not always easy but it is important. Knowing where your parent is living and knowing how and when you are going to see him or her will help you feel more secure in the middle of all the changes.

> **EXERCISE**
> Put your name in the centre circle of the family tree on the page opposite and write the names of your parents, brothers, sisters, grandparents, cousins, aunts, uncles, etc. in the circles around you. Look at your family. It is still the same. Your family has not changed. What has changed is your parents' relationship to each other, not to you. They will always be your parents.

SEPARATED BUT STILL LIVING TOGETHER

Parents will sometimes separate but stay living in the same house, living very separate lives.

This arrangement is a really difficult one to live with and makes it very hard not to get caught up in being the 'messenger' between your parents. You might find that each parent will, either subtly or clearly, try and get you on his or her 'side'. They may feel justified in telling you lots of information when, in fact, it would be better for you to be allowed to step back from issues that are actually theirs to work out. The ideas in this book will help you work through many issues that you will be dealing with, whether your parents are living in the same or different homes.

> 'Our house was a place without talking and communicating. No one showed an interest in anything about each other. We just lived and slept in the same house. We were a family but it never felt like that.' JULIE (15)

> 'The silence in our house was awful. Mum and Dad had separated for years but we all lived in the same house. No one shouted but no one talked. You couldn't go anywhere in the house without an atmosphere. I stayed out as much as possible to just keep away from it all.' DONÁL (16)

> 'My parents separated but stayed living in the same house for three years. They never talked to each other so I was the one telling them everything. I just got used to it. When they were able to get different places to live they were both much happier but I found it really difficult. The atmosphere hadn't been great, but at least I had them both around me.' MARIE (14)

When parents separate the huge sense of grief that you experience can be similar to that experienced as the result of a death. However, there is one very significant difference: you still have both your parents.

If there is a death in the family then children usually get lots of support and understanding from family and everyone around them, which is important and necessary.

In the case of family separation, you can miss out on much of this support. Friends don't know what is going on and so you get very little understanding or support from them (and none if you haven't even told them). The wider family of relations often has no idea of how to cope or deal with your parents separating. Rather than offering neutral support to you, they can get caught up in issues and take unhelpful 'sides'. In school you have to go in and deal with each day as you had done before, even though it feels like your life has totally changed.

However, you still have both your parents. It is important to try and keep a good relationship with each of them.

> *Just because your parents don't get on with each other and separate does not mean that they stop loving you. Give yourself time to adjust to the new situation at home. Remember it will take some effort on your part too.*

TIPS FOR COPING

- Find someone you can trust and talk to them.
- Be honest about what you are feeling and talk it through with someone.
- Don't 'bottle' things up – you have a right to be feeling as you do, but you have a responsibility (and a challenge) to yourself to make good choices. Talking is one of them. Speaking up is the best way to help yourself.
- Stay in touch with your friends – don't stop meeting up with them. Don't put off having them back to your house for too long. It may feel uncomfortable at first, but it will get easier.

- Write a diary or message board to yourself. It is good to be able to see that, while one day might get a 2/10 rating, other days get 8/10. Things change.
- Keep up with any sports teams or clubs that you belong to. Try and keep to the same routine you had before.
- Give yourself a mental break from the situation at times. Read a good book; go out and watch a match; watch a DVD; challenge a friend to a game on a playstation; listen to music; go to the cinema; go window shopping; spend time on the computer; or call a friend.
- Difficult as it may be, let go of the dream of your parents getting back together again. It is not something you can control.
- Stop and think about the good and bad consequences of any choices you can make. For example, if you stay in your room all the time and keep yourself from being around people, then the good consequence might be that you have some 'space'. The bad consequence is that you have too much space and become lonely and more upset.
- Give yourself time to adjust to the family changes. It does not all get sorted out in a few days or weeks.

Coping at School

2

School, studies and homework are enough to keep up with at the best of times. Social and sporting commitments are probably even higher up on your list of priorities. There is usually enough going on without adding any more to the list. Having to cope with parents separating on top of everything can throw you off balance. There will be days when you feel there is too much going on to handle and your mind will be in overdrive trying to sort everything out. On days like these, concentrating on work in school can be really difficult. This is quite normal at a stressful time.

To everyone else you look the same as you did the day before. No one sees anything different about you. The fact of knowing that your parents are separating has changed you on the inside, but this is not visible to your friends.

CONCENTRATION...

Concentrating on schoolwork is not easy when there is so much 'stuff' circling inside your head. Staying focused in class is difficult. Keeping yourself together can take 100 per cent effort, which does not leave much head space for trying to memorise a math formula or history dates. Having a friend you can talk to about how you are getting on at home will help clear some head space.

> '*I started to find it really hard to concentrate in class. I never used to find it hard. The teachers kept telling me to pay attention and stop daydreaming. I definitely wasn't daydreaming. I just couldn't clear my head of all that was going on at home. Everything was changing. It kind of took over my brain.*' EMER (15)

> '*My parents had shouting matches in front of us, usually about money. In class I would sit there trying to work out all their problems and worrying about what I had heard. I just couldn't get it out of my head.*' PETER (14)

IT IS BETTER FOR YOU TO LET YOUR SCHOOL KNOW

Personal information is something most of us are reluctant to talk about. Schools, however, encourage parents to let them know that a family situation is changing or has changed. Teachers understand that family separation is not an easy time for anyone. Believe it or not, it is a good thing for a parent to speak to someone in your school and tell them that things at home are changing. It might not be what you want, but your parents will want to make sure that you are supported in school at this time. You can help them decide who to speak to.

> *Letting a teacher know what is going on at home is helpful. Teachers want to support you in school during difficult times. Teachers supporting you in school doesn't mean they will be involved with what's going on at home.*

If you want to or feel able to tell the school yourself, choose a tutor or teacher who you feel you can trust and let them know that things at home are difficult. Some teenagers have said that it was easier to speak to their school guidance counsellors or to someone who did not teach them in a regular class.

> *You do not have to give lots of details.*

Talking to a staff member is not easy and you may feel uncomfortable. However, it means that a person at school can support you and be more understanding during this complicated time in your life.

> 'It was OK that my form teacher knew. He never asked questions but I felt that, if I had a disaster in school, he would understand a bit more.' JOHN (17)

> 'My mum rang my school and told them about her and Dad separating, but she never told me she had done that. I was really embarrassed and uncomfortable when my form teacher asked me if I was OK. I should have been told that she knew – that would have been better.' SUSAN (13)

EXTRA RESPONSIBILITIES

You might be at a stage in your life when you feel you are just starting to enjoy a little more independence. Just when you begin to think that your life is becoming more your own, you can find that you need to adjust your routine and plans because of the family changes. There will be times when you can depend on others in the family and different times when they need to be able to depend on you. It is a two-way process. Talking together and trying to work out solutions to some practical issues at home is not always easy, but it is a part of family life. Different solutions should be considered, rather than assuming there is only one answer, or none at all.

DAVID'S STORY

'Before my parents separated, I got up for school at the last minute, grabbed everything that I needed and just did my own thing. Now Mum leaves for work earlier and I have to get my little brother and sister up and ready for school too – I have a list in the mornings. Recently, I was late for school and was given a detention. I was so mad. I don't think I should have been punished for being late. Anyone would have been late if they had to do all that I did.' DAVID (14)

It seems that David was working hard at home to try and help his mum out with his younger brother and sister in the mornings. He found he didn't have enough time to do everything and was often late for school. He couldn't see any solution and didn't want his mum to have any more pressures, so he didn't tell her. No one in school knew that his parents had separated and so David had no support there. Things bottled up inside him and it was not until he lost his temper in school and yelled abuse at a teacher that the problem was recognised.

David and his mum came up with a plan to do some things the night before and everyone set their alarms fifteen minutes earlier. Instead of David feeling that he was responsible for everything, his mum made it clear that he was not responsible for her being OK. Talking about it together and being honest helped David put things into perspective.

David wrote a letter of apology to the teacher in school and did the detention, but felt relieved that the school understood his situation. He also told a friend on his soccer team whose parents were separated, so at least he had one person who understood what he was going through.

DON'T HIDE THE FACT THAT YOUR PARENTS ARE SEPARATED

Some people try and convince themselves that they are the only ones this is happening to. This is just not true and will leave you feeling worse if you believe it.

JOE'S STORY
'When I started secondary school I didn't tell anyone my parents were separated. My sports bag was a problem because I had to bring it in on Tuesdays (even though games weren't until Wednesday) since I stayed at Dad's on Tuesday nights. The lads would laugh at me as though I was stupid. I used to hate Tuesdays and going to Dad's because of that. I couldn't tell Mum or Dad because they would just say I was being silly. They didn't understand. Just because they had separated a few years ago they thought everything was fine ... but this was a new school and it mattered to me.' JOE (12)

Joe's sports bag caused him the most upset. Trying to keep his parents' separation a secret in his new secondary school was making his life miserable, especially on Tuesdays. At such times you have to stop and think through what are the consequences, positive and negative, of your decisions. By keeping his parents' separation secret, Joe faced hassle each Tuesday. He also got mad with his mum most Tuesday mornings and started to resent going to see his dad because of the problems it caused him.

Everything was resolved when Joe decided to be open about having two homes. Nobody took much notice and, after a while, people stopped commenting that he brought his bag in a day early. Talking issues through with your parents, or another close relative or friend, is a good way of reaching solutions.

> **Having separated parents is nothing to be ashamed of.**

Stephen and Áine went through most of secondary school hiding the fact that their parents had separated. You might be interested in their comments.

> *'I didn't want anybody in school to know that my parents were separated. I didn't want to answer questions, but more important was the fact that I did not want people treating me differently or looking at me with sympathy. I couldn't bear that. So I kept quiet and put in a lot of effort keeping the fact a secret. Later on [in fifth year] I realised that a lot of people knew anyway and that nobody had treated me differently because of it. When I did talk about it I found out that five other boys in my form were from separated families – we had been in school together for years and none of us had ever talked about our families being separated until then.'* **STEPHEN (17)**

> *'I didn't tell anyone that my parents had separated until I was in sixth year. I started to worry about my school graduation and how I was going to manage both my parents wanting to be there. I eventually told my friends why I was so upset and they couldn't understand why I had never told them before. It was such a relief to be able to talk about it. I realised it had been a mistake keeping it secret all those years in school. It wouldn't have changed any of my friendships and would have made life better for me.'* **ÁINE (17)**

TRUST A FRIEND AND TELL HIM OR HER

You might decide to tell just one friend until you have had time to come to terms with things yourself. It really does help to have someone to talk to who will listen. You definitely won't be just talking about your family all the time. However, knowing you can does make a difference.

> *Friends can give you great support just by knowing what you are going through and understanding that some days are difficult. Friends remind you that you are OK, even though the situation may not be.*

'I only told my closest friend in school. I didn't want everyone knowing. Having someone to talk to helped. It also helped that everyone wasn't talking about it around me.' NUALA (15)

School can actually give you a break from everything that's going on at home. Doing your homework at a friend's house after school or going to the school or local library to study, especially around exam times, can help you concentrate more easily. Some schools have after-school study. If you have exams coming up, it may be worth checking out if you can stay behind after school for this.

'It was really important for me to keep school and home separate. I trained myself to walk out of the house in the morning and leave "that lot" behind and just go to school. It was how I managed things. When I got home and came back in the door I was walking into a different part of my life. School helped me to forget.' JANET (16)

ENERGY EXERCISE

> This is something to think about, particularly if your parents have separated recently.
>
> List some things that were part of your life before your parents' separation.
>
> Suggested list:
> - School/study
> - Family/home
> - Job
> - Church activities
> - Sports
> - Scouts or other club
> - Music and other interests
> - Friends
>
> Let's say that each person is given tokens for ten units of energy a day. How did your ten units of time and energy get divided up before you heard about your parents separating? Write a number next to each relevant item. Make sure the total does not exceed ten.
>
> Now write the list again but, instead of the word 'family', write separately 'Mum', 'Dad' and 'home'. Energy units are not just spent doing things, but also thinking about things. A lot of mental energy can be used up by thinking about what is going on at home and in the family. Write down how your ten units are used up since your parents separated. Compare your lists. Has anything changed? Look at how much energy you used in the first list under 'family/home' and compare it with the second list and the combined score of 'Mum', 'Dad' and 'Home'. Is anything different?

We all only have a certain amount of energy to use each day and we rarely stop to think about how we use it. There will be days when you will feel totally exhausted and not feel like doing the things that you have easily done before. It can be a real struggle to concentrate in school, play and enjoy sport, or even socialise with your friends. This is normal.

Looking at your energy chart will help you understand what has changed. Thinking about your parents and the family situation can take over and use up most of your energy. Other parts of your life may run low on energy.

GETTING THE BALANCE BACK

Deciding how you use your energy is not always straightforward, but you do have some control. Keeping everything bottled up and not talking to anyone will make it harder to regain the balance.

It is important to have a life outside of your family as well as within it. If you are involved in outside interests, activities, hobbies or are a member of a club, then make sure you keep it up. Let one of the leaders or coaches know about home so that they will understand why your concentration or attendance may be a little irregular for a while. If you are not comfortable telling them yourself, then suggest that one of your parents calls or talks to them. Just because your parents are separated doesn't mean that you can't go out and have some fun or a laugh. Your parents will want to see that you can get on with your life in a positive way.

Be patient with yourself. It takes time to adjust. It takes time to work things out.

> *Your family life is changing – not ending.*
> *Stop and think about what you have that is a positive thing in your life. Don't get in a habit of just seeing what is wrong.*

TIPS FOR SCHOOL

- You are not alone. Every class, form and year in any school across Ireland will have students from separated homes.
- Trust a friend and talk to them about your parents separating.
- Tell someone on the school staff. He or she will be supportive, not intrusive.
- It is normal to find concentrating in school difficult with all that is going on. Talking about some of your concerns with a parent or another adult will help with this problem. It will take time.
- If you are close to exams, see if it is possible to do some study in your local library or to stay for after-school study.
- Stay involved in any sports or after-school activities.
- Keep up with your friends – don't stop seeing them.
- If extra responsibilities, either before or after school, are affecting your schoolwork, then your parents will want to know.
- Do the 'energy exercise' every now and then and keep a check that things stay balanced.
- Having parents that are separated is nothing to be ashamed of or embarrassed about.

Stuck in the Middle

'My parents used me to send messages to each other. It was like being a postman with a registered letter. I had to make sure they got a message but, if it wasn't something they wanted to receive, I got all their emotions and anger dumped on me. It wasn't fair.' RORY (13)

'I found it difficult with my mum and dad not speaking to each other. I was sometimes given horrible messages to pass between them. The worst of these were about money. It made me feel really uncomfortable and angry. I wanted to tell them to "grow up" but I didn't.' PAT (17)

'I think parents should be made to keep in touch with each other, and find a way to communicate about us kids without us being the messengers.' MAEVE (14)

THE ROLE OF MESSENGER

CONOR'S STORY

> 'I used to see myself as a bridge between my parents ... a bit like a rope bridge linking two very steep rocky sides with a huge drop below.' CONOR (16)

Conor's parents had separated and he was very aware of the huge gulf between them when they refused to talk to or acknowledge each other. Conor believed that, if he could keep going carefully to and fro across the bridge, at some point they would start crossing the bridge themselves and begin to talk to each other. But, according to Conor:

> 'I got it wrong. They have never managed to really talk to each other properly again. Me running back and forwards across it was useless. I was the only one on it. In the end I just got on with trying to have as good a relationship as I could with them individually, and left them to get on with whatever communication or non-communication they decided for themselves.'

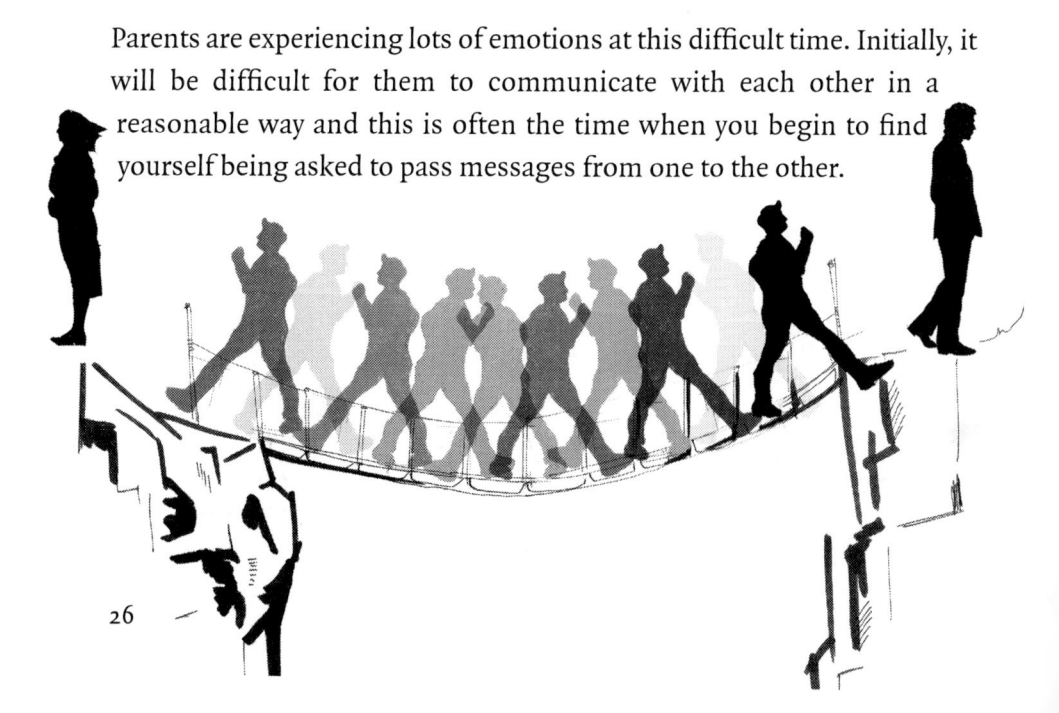

Parents are experiencing lots of emotions at this difficult time. Initially, it will be difficult for them to communicate with each other in a reasonable way and this is often the time when you begin to find yourself being asked to pass messages from one to the other.

If you become the messenger between your parents then you will shortly find yourself caught up in the crossfire between them. Messages you bring will often be misunderstood and misinterpreted. You might even find yourself accused of taking sides.

> 'Parents should allow their children to be neutral.' **MARTIN (16)**

At some point you will face pressure to be more loyal to one parent over the other. Sometimes this pressure comes from your parents and at other times there can be pressure from within yourself, based on information that you have been given. You will feel divided and torn between them both. It's important to try not to take sides. This creates a dilemma as both your parents will be looking to you for support. It will be a struggle and will take a lot of effort to stay neutral and not get caught up in issues that belong to your parents and only they can sort out.

Having to decide when to give the message or worrying about the response will give you a lot of unnecessary stress. It is not good for you to be caught in the middle like this.

Your parents may not have realised that they are putting you in an impossible position (they are usually preoccupied with trying to avoid a difficult situation for themselves). Choosing not to be the 'go-between' can be difficult, but it is possible. Help your parents understand by explaining to them what it is like for you being put in this position. You may have to tell both parents so neither feels less important in your life.

You could say something like: 'I feel that you are putting me in a really difficult situation when you ask me to pass these messages between you both and it makes me feel uncomfortable. I think it would be better for me not to do it.'

Letting your parents know what this is like for you is really important. It is the only way they will know. In all the family changes there is something that stays the same – *you matter*. You matter to your parents and your happiness is important to them. It is good to find your voice and be able to talk to them about the things that are important to you and how you are feeling.

> **EXERCISE**
> *Get three table tennis balls or something similar and put a pair of eyes on each one. Put one ball facing the other ball with a gap in the middle. These represent your parents. Now put the third ball in the middle of the row. This is you. You might want to look straight ahead and be neutral, but when you are given a message you need to turn your ball to face that parent. Then turn the ball back again in the other direction to your other parent and relay the message to them. As you constantly do this you might realise that you are the only ball that is doing any of the work.*
>
> *Now place the three balls in a triangle. Your ball is the top of the triangle. Turn the other two balls to face you.*

> *What do you notice? Actually, you can see both of them from where you are. You can communicate with each parent directly. You can do this and be an equal space from both of them. Your parents must decide how to communicate across the space between them. It is not your job to be in that space.*

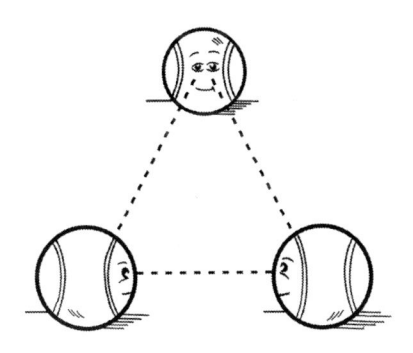

Staying neutral means that you can more easily stay out of issues that are not your responsibility. Suggest to your parents that they could text each other rather than use you to pass messages between them.

THE ROLE OF PRIVATE DETECTIVE

Private Detective: someone who carries out investigations on someone's behalf privately.

If you drop the job of being a messenger between your parents, you might next find yourself being given the new job of private detective.

'When Mum and Dad stopped living together each still wanted to know what the other was doing. I didn't mind the odd question but then it started to really annoy me. I felt I was being used just to get information and it spoiled things for me. If they wanted to know this stuff, they should have just asked each other.'
SINÉAD (15)

'Dad was asking me questions about home and was anything different, and I told him we got a new TV. He went really mad and started saying that he was giving Mum too much money if she was able to go out and get a new TV. He was really angry. I just felt that it had nothing to do with me, how they worked out money. I also decided that I was not going to be a spy in each camp anymore and give either of them any information on the other house.' DAMIEN (16)

'Mum was convinced that Dad was seeing someone else and wanted me to "check things out" while I was with him at his place. I felt really uncomfortable being there and doing that, and it started to spoil the relationship between me and my dad because I wasn't relaxed and being myself. It spoiled my relationship with my mum as well because she felt I wasn't supporting her by telling her things. In the end I told my mum that this would have to change as I couldn't deal with it anymore. I stopped going to my dad's for a while, but that wasn't what I wanted to happen. I decided to take things into my own hands and stop being Mum's private detective. It made things difficult between me and Mum for a while, but then things settled down.' ORLAITH (18)

JOB OFFER

The detective is sent on assignment to spy on the other parent's house and is expected to report back with his or her observations on:

- Who was there.
- What they said about ....(any subject).

- Whether he or she is seeing anybody else.
- If anything new had been bought.
- If anything was different.

If you are being used as a private detective for a parent then get ready for lots of questions. Some of them may be straightforward, but constant questions and questioning leaves you feeling fed-up and frustrated. In these circumstances you will get pulled into a 'conflict of loyalties'. You care about your parents and want to be loyal to both of them. Wearing a detective badge, however, puts you in a difficult and uncomfortable position. You want to answer the questions because it seems unreasonable not to and yet you don't want to be talking or giving information or 'evidence' that can be used against you or the other parent. This is another time to use your courage and find your voice to speak up.

Parents often don't realise that their questions are making things difficult for you. Your parents will have spent years living closely together and sharing a lot of details about each others daily lives. Adjusting to not knowing or having answers to these same details will take time for them too. You can help them understand by explaining that you love them both and want to have the best possible relationship with each of them. This means having their permission to spend time with each of them without any expectations from the other about giving reports back. It can take a while for the habit to break and you may need to be very patient.

> *Remember: when you spend time with your parents, your relationship to each of them is as a son or daughter. Leave the detective badge behind and be yourself.*

PARENTS WANT YOU TO TALK, NOT PRETEND

- Mum and Dad have enough worries.
- I don't know if I can find the right words.
- It will cause more trouble.
- They won't understand.
- If I say nothing they will think I'm OK.

Talking to your parents can sometimes be difficult, especially if it is about how you are feeling regarding some of the things going on in the family at the moment. Finding the right words is not always easy. Sometimes finding reasons to convince yourself not to talk is easier than talking. Some reasons not to talk can be:

- 'They won't understand.'
- 'They have enough worries without me telling them mine as well.'
- 'I don't think I can explain it.'
- 'I have no idea how or where to start talking.'
- 'Things are sort of OK at the moment and I don't want to rock the boat.'
- 'What I'm upset about does not seem important compared to what they are dealing with.' (Like paying for your school trip when they are worrying about the house bills.)
- 'I might get upset if I start talking.'

You can decide to say nothing and tell everyone that you are 'fine' if they ask. Eventually things will build up and this won't help you or your parents. It can be like a volcano – no one can see what is going on under the surface until it erupts. You may be used to volcanoes erupting in your house, but the secret of good communication in a family is facing and dealing with issues in an honest and respectful way – and dealing with them as they come along, not storing up a year's supply.

> *Parents assume that you are getting on fine simply because you are not telling them anything different.*

You might believe that, because you are a teenager and not a young child anymore, you should manage everything on your own. Parents can misread your silence and believe that you are OK. They can't see behind your mask to know that you are not as OK as you are pretending to be. Being honest with yourself and with them, and talking to one of them is essential. You are important to your parents. They need your help in understanding how things really are for you today.

You will find some 'Tips for Talking' at the end of Chapter 4.

Dealing with Your Anger 4

Is it OK to get angry?	**Yes**
Is it OK to feel anger?	**Yes**
Is it OK to be angry with the changes in your family?	**Yes**
Is it OK to express anger?	**Yes**

Anger is something everyone has to deal with. It is an important emotion and can be something positive because it activates you to do something in a situation. Feeling angry is OK. What is not OK is if the anger takes control and changes your behaviour. Learning to control anger rather than allowing anger to control you is challenging. It's not easy – but it is possible.

Anger is a normal feeling, but some of its effects are not always positive.

Anger can:

- Make your mind exaggerate situations.
- Make you sleep badly.
- Make your body tense.
- Make you waste opportunities to talk to your parents because you're acting out the anger rather than responding to it.

How would someone know that you are angry? Do you curl up in a corner on your own like a hedgehog with all the spikes sticking out so that you are left alone? Or are you like a rhinoceros that stamps its foot before charging into the middle of things?

The rhino and the hedgehog scenarios are unhelpful reactions to feeling angry. The challenge is to work out how to respond to anger rather than just react to it. Anger is the feeling and behaviour is the choice.

CHALLENGE: LEARN HOW TO RESPOND AND NOT JUST REACT TO YOUR ANGER

So, what makes you angry? Sometimes it is easy knowing why you are angry. Perhaps you are feeling frustrated at your plans being changed, at being blamed for something that is not your fault or at having to do extra jobs at home when you feel you have enough to do anyway. At other times you can feel angry and upset without knowing exactly what it is that is making you feel that way just at that moment.

Chapter 1 looked at how you are feeling. Many of these feelings are often related to anger. Underneath the exterior of 'I'm OK' can lie a lot of anger and bitterness that your family life has been altered and changed dramatically. Perhaps you feel hurt or let down by someone close to you. When you experience a sense of powerlessness and helplessness in a situation and don't know what is happening, then all these emotions can rise to the surface and show themselves as anger. Sometimes anger is there because we can feel afraid in a situation and don't know what to do.

WARNING! Stop and identify what it is that is making you feel so unhappy.

Triggers to anger:

- Disappointment
- Fear
- Sadness
- Anxiety
- Embarrassment
- Frustration
- Rejection
- Jealousy
- Shame

... and there are many more.

> *A positive effect of anger is that it lets you know something is not right. A negative effect of anger is that it can take away your reasoning skills (and sometimes your common sense). Identifying the causes behind the anger will help you talk about it and deal with the reasons for it.*

DON'T BOTTLE THINGS UP

Repress: to hide a thought or feeling; not expressing things openly and keeping them in your mind.

> **Stop** repressing
> **Start** expressing

Repressing anger or putting a mask on is not a good idea. It's also unfair and dishonest to yourself and those around you. Controlling how you appear to everyone and pretending you are OK does not make anger disappear.

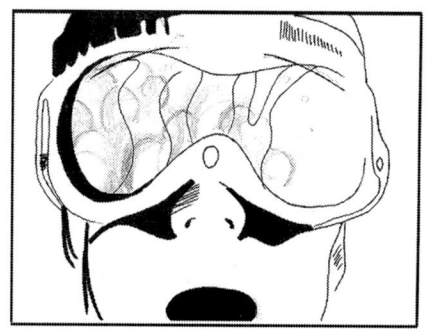

An avalanche of snow can cause huge destruction and, if you have any sense, you will get out of its path fast. It may have been started by something small which then triggers a mass movement of snow. Anger, similarly, has a habit of starting small. If it is ignored, it can grow to become a destructive force. Unfortunately, our family and friends and the people we care about most get hurt in the aftermath.

> ***Learning to control your anger is very different to repressing it.***

'I learned to keep quiet and calm on the outside, but inside I felt like exploding. I would go in my room and blast my music out.' JAMES (12)

'I was so angry with my dad that I decided not to talk to him. The longer it went on the harder it became. I wanted to punish him but it just made me feel miserable and I began to realise that I was punishing myself.' NINA (17)

REACTIONS TO ANGER ... THE AVALANCHE!

- Addictions
- Bad Temper
- Outrage
- Silence
- Bitterness
- Sarcasm
- Disgruntlement
- Violence
- Rage
- Depression
- Resentment
- Cruel Gossip
- Hostility
- Anti-social Behaviour

ANGER

The illustration on the previous page shows some reactions we have to anger. You may identify with many of them. The problem is that, when you only react to the anger and don't learn to respond and deal with it appropriately, then your life can get pretty miserable. Your school, friends and parents then react to your outbursts and attitude. You and the behaviour are seen as the problems, while the real issues get unresolved. It is a vicious circle.

There are three ways we can respond to the situations and people around us. We can be:

(a) Passive
(b) Aggressive
(c) Assertive

A passive answer or response to someone might sound like:

'Forget I said anything.'
'It doesn't matter.'
'It's probably all my fault.'
'I don't know what came over me.'
Silence

An aggressive response might be:

'You'd better.'
'Shut up.'
'You'll be sorry.'
'Get lost.'
'I'll get you back.'
'Watch out.'
' *******!'

An assertive response is:

'I think ...'
'In my opinion ...'
'I don't like ...'
'I get frustrated when ...'
'I am angry about ...'
'I would like to ...'

(A) PASSIVE BEHAVIOUR

Passive: not expressing your own feelings, needs, ideas; ignoring your own rights; allowing others to infringe on your rights.

If you react passively, you are hoping it will all work out OK, while keeping quiet about what you really think. You don't stand up for yourself, say what you think or get what you want.

(B) AGGRESSIVE BEHAVIOUR

Aggressive: expressing your feelings, needs and ideas at the expense of others; standing up for your rights but ignoring the rights of others; trying to dominate, even humiliate others.

If you react aggressively, you argue, make threats and upset other people until you get your own way. You act like a bully. You don't care about the rights or feelings of other people. It is a case of 'all take and no give'.

(C) ASSERTIVE BEHAVIOUR

Assertive: expressing your feelings, needs and ideas. Standing up for your genuine and legitimate rights in ways that do not disregard the rights of others.

Assertive behaviour means you say what you want and how you feel. You know your rights and the rights of others. You don't want to win at any price. You also don't assume that people can read your mind.
(SOURCE: Teen Between®)

Learning how to communicate at a time when you are angry or upset is not easy. Even with practice it is still difficult and no one gets it right all the time. Remember that communicating honestly is important.

Maybe you have never stopped to think about how anger affects you or how you actually deal with it. As you move from being a child to a young adult it is helpful to work out some of these issues for yourself. You are in the driver's seat for deciding the direction you take.

Think about how you might react in a given situation.
What is your usual reaction?
What are the consequences for you and for those around you?

When you let people know what you are thinking in an honest and respectful way, it prevents anger building up under the surface. Talking things through will help you understand a situation more clearly. If you understand more clearly, and feel more understood, this will help change things.

Remember that listening is important too. Be prepared to listen to other people's opinions and thoughts on the situation. You will often see things differently and you might not agree, but that is OK. Remember that listening is not just waiting for your turn to talk.

BE PART OF THE SOLUTION, NOT PART OF THE PROBLEM

Here are some pointers:

- It will take effort on your part to try and understand your parents' perspective. You do not have to agree with each other, but you do have to try and understand each other.

- You can't expect people to know what you are thinking. You will need to help them to understand things from your perspective.

- Every action has a consequence.

- Your understanding of a situation will affect your feelings and reactions to it. As well as wanting to be understood, you need to take time to listen and to understand.

- It makes a difference if you apologise to your parents when you have reacted inappropriately.

- Rebelling against your parents might seem easier than talking to them. Choosing to do this and making bad choices could be your way of getting back at them. This will just lead to you and your family being unhappy. You can convince yourself that this is OK, but it won't make you happier.

- When you are thinking ahead about what you want to say, it may help to write it down and read it aloud to hear yourself saying it.
- Parents are people too. They are people who can and will make mistakes and get things wrong. Being willing to forgive, and asking for forgiveness when you need to, are great building blocks in a relationship.

Remember that talking about things and finding out clearer information can totally change our view and how we feel about something. I was recently involved in a job with three builders. Two did all the work while the third person, the foreman, appeared to do very little work other than instructing the other two and sitting drinking tea.

I started to feel very frustrated and annoyed with the foreman. During a conversation with him, however, he showed me a recent scar that went from his ear right around his neck where he had had recent head surgery. He was currently working as a favour to his boss in order to train the two apprentices working on the job. This information gave me a very different understanding of the situation and the anger and frustration disappeared.

> *Changing our thinking can, at times, give us the ability to let go of our anger.*

LETTING ANGER OUT

It is important to let anger out in ways that will not hurt you or other people.

We all have 'warning signs' in ourselves when we begin to feel angry. Examples are tapping a foot, biting nails, raising eyebrows, the sensation of our stomachs knotting or increased heart rate.

It is important to become aware of what your own warning signs are. When a warning sign appears ... stop. Take three long, slow deep breaths. Slowing down your breathing does help.

Think about what is going on for you in that moment and situation. Take a little time to think about how you can respond and talk about it, rather than just reacting to it. Talk and get more information. Keep your own self respect and stay respectful to others. Be willing to consider different ideas around the issue.

Proceed with caution. When you take a little time out to notice the warning signs and proceed more carefully you will, hopefully, start getting an internal message saying, 'It is safe to continue.'

EXERCISE
What are your warning signs that you are getting angry?

Write them down here:
1.
2.
3.

EXERCISE

Sometimes we talk about anger as though it is something in us that has to get out. There is often a real sense of things building up inside us and below are some ideas to help release some of the anger that you can at times experience. It is not a full list. Find ways that are best for you and add your own suggestions.

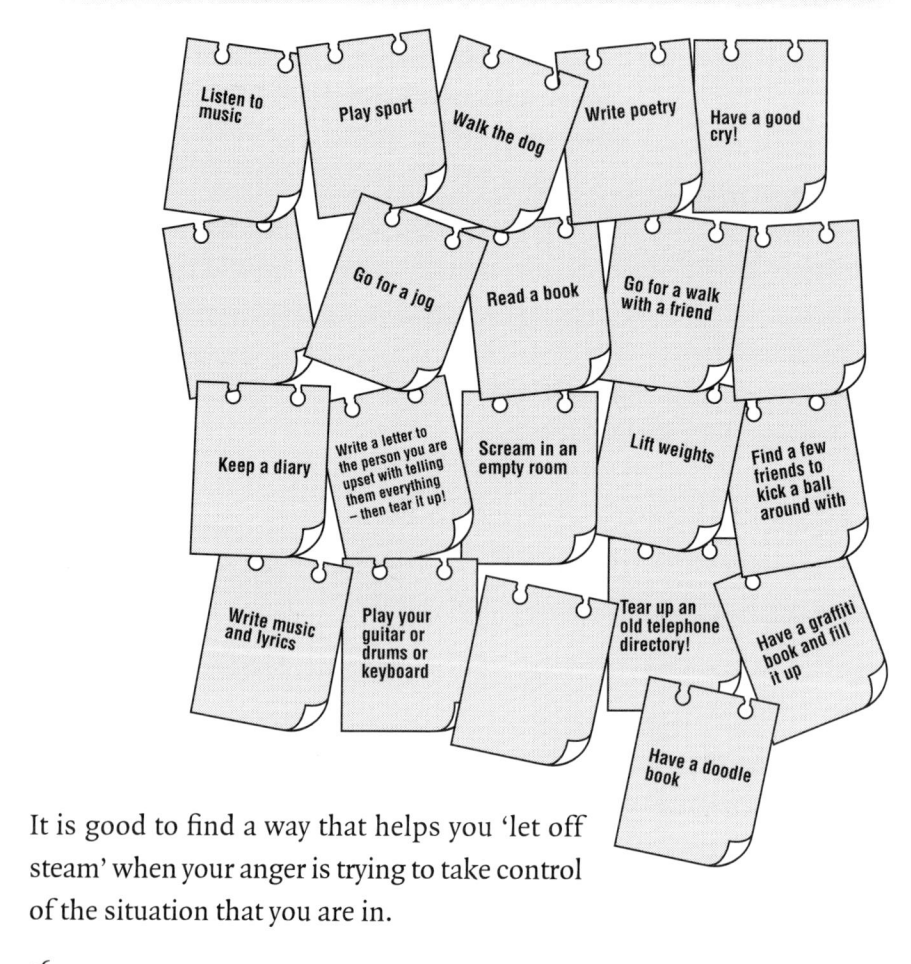

- Listen to music
- Play sport
- Walk the dog
- Write poetry
- Have a good cry!
- Go for a jog
- Read a book
- Go for a walk with a friend
- Keep a diary
- Write a letter to the person you are upset with telling them everything – then tear it up!
- Scream in an empty room
- Lift weights
- Find a few friends to kick a ball around with
- Write music and lyrics
- Play your guitar or drums or keyboard
- Tear up an old telephone directory!
- Have a graffiti book and fill it up
- Have a doodle book

It is good to find a way that helps you 'let off steam' when your anger is trying to take control of the situation that you are in.

> *Talk things through with someone who knows you well and who also understands the circumstances.*
> *Be careful that this friend does not take the brunt of your anger or he/she may not stay around to support you the next time.*

Parents can find it hard to recognise and accept that you are growing up. This can be frustrating. You should talk to your parents, but be mature in the way you talk to them and reach a compromise. When you are talking:

- Stay calm.
- Stay cool.
- Stay respectful.

TIPS FOR TALKING

- Stop. Take three deep breaths.
- Think about what you want to say.
- Deal with one issue at a time – target the issue and not the person.
- Be honest about what is bothering you and why you are upset.
- Listen to the other person's thinking too. Share the time to talk and listen.
- You will be asked questions, so be prepared with good answers.
- Be aware of your own body language.
- Admit when you are wrong about something.

- Be willing to forgive your parent or other person.
- Agree to discuss something and think about it. Decisions can be made later.
- Be willing to compromise. Being part of a family means taking other people's needs into account as well as your own.
- Be clear and agree on any actions or plans that you decide together.

Understanding Your Parents' Distress

5

I wonder if you have realised just how different your needs are from your parents' needs at times? This is especially true when they first separate. You will see from the table on the following page that there are many times when your reaction to things can be very different to theirs. The problem with this is that parents assume your needs are the same as theirs and you assume that your parents need the same things as you.

'I wish my parents would realise that I don't see things the way they do. They assume their opinion is right and never bother to ask me what I think.'

TIM (13)

DIFFERENCES

The table below will help you understand how you and your parents might be looking at the same situation and reacting to it in different ways. When you have had time to look at it, you might find it helps to show it to your parents and talk about it together.

HOW PARENTS SEE THINGS	HOW YOU SEE THINGS
One parent wants to try and emotionally detach from the other parent. This is not easy for them and it takes a long time to adjust to not being in a couple.	You need to stay emotionally attached to both of your parents. You need to keep in regular contact with them both (except in exceptional circumstances).
Parents need to accept that their marriage is over. Again this is easier said than done.	You may hope and believe that they will get back together.
Parents need time to readjust to the changes and decide what to do next.	You need your life to return to some kind of normal routine. Knowing the plans and arrangements helps.
Parents accept that the separation is an ending and rejection of their own relationship, but not a rejection of the children.	You may sometimes feel rejected because your parents are separating and are not able to stay living together with you.
Parents can assume that their children want something to change if their parents are unhappy and always arguing.	You may be so used to your parents arguing that you see no reason why their separation will make things better.
Adults who have been in an unhappy marriage might hope to find happiness in a new relationship.	You may not share this opinion, especially if you feel that this new relationship was a reason for the breakdown of your parents' marriage.
Parents can sometimes believe that separation/divorce will give them a second chance.	You may not see your parents' separation in the same way.

(Source: Teen Between ®)

GRIEF

'It was only after they separated that I really thought about my parents and whether they were actually OK or not. It was awful seeing Mum cry one minute and then have her shouting at us the next. None of us knew what to do. I was just scared that she wouldn't cope because she was the one who always looked after us.' SUE (16)

'I really worried about my dad after he and Mum separated. He got really quiet and a bit weird. He had always been great fun but he seemed to change. It felt like he was sulking, but I guess he was just upset about everything that was going on. I just wish he could have made more of an effort when I did see him. I found out from someone that Dad's reactions were normal. It made me feel a little better knowing that he just needed some time.' TONY (13)

'One day my little brother made some stupid joke and we all fell around laughing. It was good because it seemed like we had all stopped laughing in our house after Mum and Dad separated. It was like we left our sense of humour outside the house because it didn't seem appropriate. It was a relief to laugh again.' GERRY (17)

'I think my dad feels everyone is against him when actually I am really worried and upset about him.' ALAN (12)

'Everyone thinks I am coping really well – but inside I know I'm not.'
JOANNA (14)

Every family member will need time to adjust to the changes that are happening in the family after the separation. Grief and sadness affect everyone differently, but there are some common reactions to grief. You might have recognised some of these in your parents and worried about them.

These are all normal reactions to grief:

- Emotional exhaustion (making them appear distant).
- Sleeplessness and therefore tiredness all the time.
- Crying.
- Sighing.
- Mood swings – from high one day to low the next.
- Difficulty in concentrating. You may be talking to them and find that they are not really hearing or following what you are saying.
- Sadness (sometimes depression).
- Anger and criticalness. This can be directed either at him/herself or at your other parent.

You will want to try and protect your parent from feeling like this, but you can't. You might read the list and recognise that you are experiencing some things yourself, for example, lack of concentration in school. It is a tough time for everyone, but it will not always be like this. Things will get better, but not overnight. It takes time and there is no fast route.

> **Remember: separation is a process and not just an event.**

'Mum kept saying that we would all have been better off if Dad had died. She said it would have made everything simpler and that we could have just got on with our lives more easily. I used to cry at night whenever I thought of this. It would never have been better if he had died. I know he doesn't live with us anymore, but he is still here and I still have my dad.' ALICE (12)

> **It may be the end of your parents' marriage – but you still have them both.**

Separation is a very stressful time for any parent. In many ways the grief and sadness that all the family experience is similar to the grief when someone dies. There are, however, some big differences between bereavement and separation.

When someone dies there is a funeral to be arranged and everyone knows about it. Friends and family come and offer support and comfort. With separation, it is usually the case that people find out gradually over time, as it is often kept a secret initially. Instead of getting support and comfort, you may find that people are uncomfortable talking about it to you. The wider family of aunts, cousins and grandparents can all start acting strangely too.

When someone dies you obviously can't see them anymore. When parents are trying to adjust to not living together as a couple it can be difficult at the beginning when they keep bumping into each other at school, shops or work. It is difficult for you too. You are seeing your parents, but things are different and you can feel different. Parents and children will adjust over different lengths of time.

THE EMOTIONAL ROLLER-COASTER RIDE

Stop and think of what it is like to be in your parents' shoes. As pointed out earlier, your family separating was never part of their plan from the beginning, so it's important to understand how difficult and upsetting the situation is for them too. It may be that only one parent wants the marriage to end. This is hard as you see one parent believing that they can only be happy by living apart and the other believing that they can only be happy by staying together.

The illustration below will help you understand some of the emotions and struggles that parents experience following their separation. Look at this and take a guess at where each of your parents might be on the graph. Remember that this is just your opinion. Think of it as a journey. Each person will have to travel along the road to get to the other end. Sometimes people get lost or stuck in one place and it can take longer before they move along. Sometimes it will seem as if they are going round in circles.

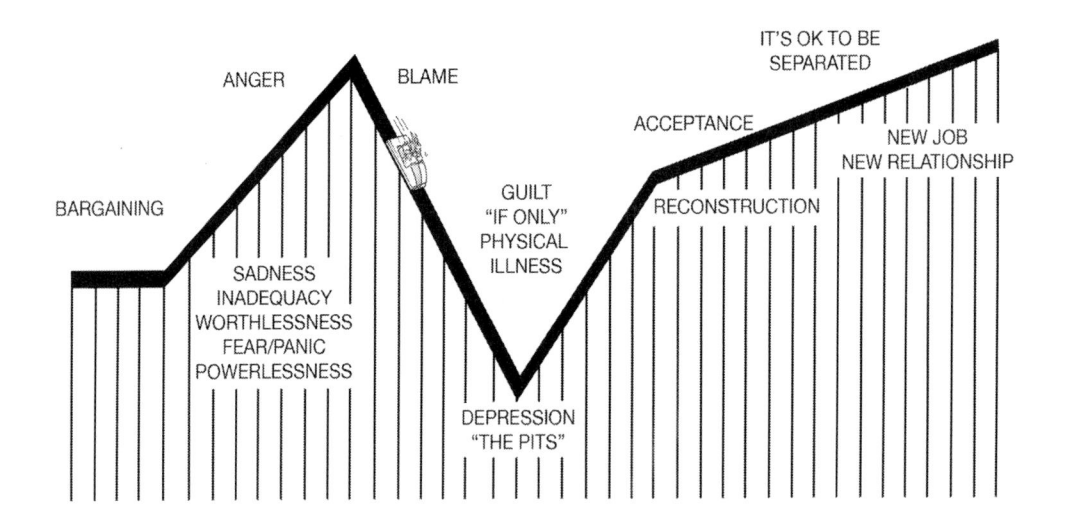

```
                    ANGER       BLAME                                    IT'S OK TO BE
                                                                         SEPARATED
                                                     ACCEPTANCE
                                                                              NEW JOB
                                                                              NEW RELATIONSHIP
                                            GUILT
BARGAINING                                  "IF ONLY"    RECONSTRUCTION
                                            PHYSICAL
                    SADNESS                 ILLNESS
                    INADEQUACY
                    WORTHLESSNESS
                    FEAR/PANIC
                    POWERLESSNESS

                                        DEPRESSION
                                        "THE PITS"
```

If your parent has been left because of another relationship, they will probably be feeling very rejected, lonely and hurt. The parent who has left the relationship, or who is in a new relationship, may also be feeling guilty and upset because of the hurt this has caused you and the family. You cannot stop them experiencing their pain.

Looking at the roller-coaster you might realise that one parent has moved more quickly along the track and adjusted to being separated in a shorter period of time, while the other parent is still struggling to accept that the relationship is over.

> *Remember: encourage your parent to talk to his or her friends or other family members for support.*

'It was quite a frightening thing to realise that I was going to have to cope with everything and everyone at home on my own. I had always been used to having another parent and adult to share the responsibility with. It took me quite a long time to adjust and stop worrying.' A PARENT

'In the first few months after we separated I had to deal with finances, legal issues, living arrangements and a lot of emotional things too. I worried about how we would all survive. I couldn't deal with my children's issues at the same time as sorting out all the other things. I didn't know how to talk about it to them. They were my priority, but I don't think they felt it.' A PARENT

'Looking back, I realise that there was so much upset and anger going on between my parents that they were not able to talk about us children at the time – they couldn't talk about anything to each other. We all wanted to know what was going to happen, but we weren't likely to get this information while they wouldn't or couldn't speak to each other.' SIOBHÁN (16)

When your parents are trying to deal with all their own emotions they will often be too upset to listen to you properly. Their comments may seem unfair or even unreasonable. This is why it is often easier to talk to someone who is not in the middle of everything. In time, things will settle down and life will have a better routine.

> *This is the start of your family living in a different way – it is not the end of your family.*

TIPS FOR COPING WITH YOUR PARENTS' DISTRESS

- Grief is a painful but unavoidable part of separation.
- You cannot stop your parent from experiencing grief and sadness.
- You are not the parent. You may be tempted to 'parent your parent' by trying to make sure he or she never feels lonely or by taking care of him or her. Kind and loving as these attempts are, they can't actually change the situation.
- Your parents want to see you getting on with your own life and keeping up with your friends. They do not want to see you staying away from things in order to mind them.
- Give your parents some time to come to terms with things too. They may not feel ready to answer all your questions when you ask them.
- If you are concerned that your parent is not coping or is unwell then speak to another adult in your wider family.
- With time, everyone will learn to adjust.
- This is the start of your family living in a different way. It is not the end of your family.

Be Yourself

If you sit and watch any drama, you will see various roles acted out. When families separate, it is like a play where the characters move away from what is written in the script and no one is sure what happens next. You can find yourself acting out a role in the family that you haven't actually chosen. Family members often compensate for someone's absence by trying to put themselves or another in that person's role.

THE RESPONSIBLE ONE

Perhaps you are now in the role of the 'Responsible One'. This role is usually given to the eldest child in the family or, if you are the eldest, you may have taken on this job yourself. Accepting responsibility is a good and positive part of moving away from childhood, but be careful about how much you take on. Remember that your parents are ultimately responsible for you.

> 'Mum was struggling and I felt I needed to help out more. Soon she was working longer hours and I started to feel that I was a full-time minder for my little brother. I couldn't go anywhere after school and, when Mum came in tired, I felt responsible for her too. I was angry, but I didn't talk about it because I couldn't see any way it could be different. I talked to my Gran one day and she talked to

Mum. Mum hadn't realised how much she had started to rely on me. In the end, we worked things out. Mum arranged for my brother to be minded some days after school. Now I get to see my friends on these days.' JULIE (15)

'Looking back, I don't think that I was ever 14, 15 or 16. I think I was treated and expected to be 18, 19 and 20 because I was the eldest.' ROB (18)

ANDREW'S STORY

Andrew was 14 and the eldest in his family. When his parents separated, he took on more and more responsibility in order (as he saw it) to help his mother cope. His greatest fear was that his mum would have a breakdown and his greatest worry was what would happen to them all if she did. He felt under huge pressure each day to make sure everything and everyone was OK. Andrew described his family life in terms of different kinds of shoes in his house.

The Boots: the boots belonged to 'the man of the house' – his dad. With his dad not living at home any more, Andrew felt that it was now his responsibility to replace his own runners with his dad's laced up, heavy boots. The problems with the boots were:

- They were too heavy.
- They didn't fit.
- They were uncomfortable.
- Once he was tied into them, they were too hard to take off, so Andrew kept them on twenty-four hours, seven days a week.

The Slippers: Andrew said he wanted to keep his mother in 'slippers'. He wanted to protect her from things and mind her. He felt that the more he could do for her, the better she would be.

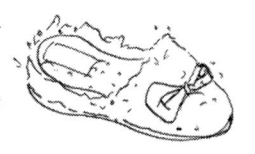

The Runners: these were the shoes Andrew saw as his own in the past, and what he hoped to wear again in the future.

The different types of shoes corresponded to the different roles in the family. Andrew realised that keeping his mother in 'slippers' was not actually helping her, long term, to live and deal with things in the present. His mother needed encouragement to get support from someone other than Andrew. The 'boots' were not Andrew's to put on. He needed to look at what he needed to do for himself in order to live at home with his family as a 14-year-old son and brother.

Andrew found that speaking with a counsellor helped him to work things out at home. It was helpful that this person was not related or involved in the family situation. Andrew began to look at what was going on and the role he was playing in his family and understood why he had begun to feel under so much pressure. Talking helped Andrew to clarify things in his own mind.

Andrew encouraged his mum to go out and talk to his aunt and another friend of hers, rather than just staying at home all the time. When his mum began to get support from wider family and friends, rather than just rely on Andrew, it helped her to cope with the situation more positively.

Talking to his mum about the pressure he felt in the mornings before school, and the responsibility of dressing his younger siblings and getting them breakfast, helped her understand Andrew's position. She acknowledged that she had been feeling a bit down and had been getting up later and later in the mornings. After talking to his mum, Andrew was reassured that she was OK. While he still helped out in the mornings, he was able to get on with things without being responsible for everything.

Changing back from boots to runners for Andrew, and from slippers back to outdoor shoes for his mother, took a little time. There were benefits for all the family in wearing shoes that fitted.

THE EMOTIONAL PROVIDER

'Will my parents be OK?' This is a real concern that many teenagers have. Needing to know that your parents are OK is one of the greatest concerns expressed following parental separation. Seeing your parents upset, hurt or distressed is very difficult. At a time when you feel you want to be cared for and comforted by your parents, it seems strange that the role is reversed and you find yourself supporting and caring for them.

Stepping into the role of the 'emotional provider' is a difficult one to avoid. Parents need huge emotional support around the time of their relationship ending (Chapter 5 might help you understand some of your parents' distress). While it is natural to want to support and comfort a parent, it can make it very hard not to get involved in issues and situations that you are not responsible for. The best thing for each parent is to find another adult that he or she can talk things through with and who they can trust. If you have taken on this role, you will find that a huge amount of your time and energy will be used up maintaining this situation.

> 'I always thought it was a positive thing that I could support my parents emotionally through their separation. Looking back, I think that I liked the fact that they relied on me. But now I want to go away to college and I am not sure how they will manage without me. I think they have grown to rely on me too much. Now it doesn't feel like such a good thing.' STUART (18)

'It felt as if both my parents were leaning on me. I was too afraid to move in case they fell down. I had no energy to do anything else.' LAURA (16)

Your parents are adults. It is important to them that you continue to get on with your own life in a good and positive way. If you are feeling responsible for them, then talk together about how you are feeling. They might see the situation very differently.

THE SISTERS' VIEWPOINT

'Mam got upset when we left her on her own at different times during the weekend. My sisters and I worked it out between us that one of us was there all the time. We didn't say anything to her – we just did it. After a while we started to argue because, although we all wanted to be there for her, we also wanted to go out.'

THE MUM'S VIEWPOINT

'Initially, it was good to know that someone was around at weekends but, as time went on, I felt I needed to stay at home because one of the girls was always there and I wanted to be there for them. One night I overheard them arguing about who was to stay in and we ended up having a good talk about a lot of things. I now plan to meet friends or family at times over the weekend and I go out more, which is better for me and for everyone. I really appreciated the love and support, but it was good to sort out together how to move on. No parent wants their children to put their own lives on hold for them.'

'PARENTING-THE-PARENT' ROLE

Sometimes you can find yourself acting the role of 'parenting your parent'. There may be times when it seems that your parents have swapped roles with you as a teenager and want to stay out late, and you are the one asking the questions about what time they will be back. From your perspective, they may be acting childishly and you might be feeling embarrassed by their behaviour. Given a little time, things will settle down and they will return to normal. They are coping with a lot of pressures and changes, and won't get everything right from the start. Talking about some of these issues needs to be done sensitively and at a calm moment, rather than at a time when they are heading out the door.

> 'Remember who the parent is and who the child is. Don't be your parents' parent.' ÁINE (17)

> 'I think I always knew that parents had to learn to let go of their children and let them be responsible for themselves. I didn't think that after my parents separated that it would be me learning to let go of my parents and letting them be responsible for themselves.' LIAM (17)

> 'At 15 I felt that I switched roles with my parents and they were the teenagers. I was minding my little sister and asking my parents when they would be back.' SIMON (15)

> 'Thinking back to the time we separated, I remember how hard I found it to deal with the children and all their questions. I know they were confused, but I was as confused as they were. Their mum and I got so caught up in our own issues that we didn't see that we were not being parents to our kids in the way they needed us to be. Separation can do that to you. I wish we had managed some things differently.' A PARENT

ROLE OF ADVOCATE

Advocate: someone who upholds or defends a cause or person; a person who intercedes on behalf of another.

Family life is obviously different when one parent is no longer living full-time in the same house as you. Just because they are not there, however, does not mean that they no longer exist. It is disappointing when you find that you can't have conversations about one parent to the other without everyone feeling awkward.

You can find yourself taking on the role of advocate for the absent parent. Instead of giving your own opinion on something, or thinking about what you feel about a situation for yourself, you start speaking on behalf of the parent who, at that time, is not present.

If you find yourself doing this, be careful. You will find yourself in the middle of arguments, none of which you want to be in, simply by trying to defend and represent your other parent.

Playing 'advocate' means that your own opinions don't get heard. Remember that you are only guessing someone else's thoughts when you try and speak on their behalf. Parents are able to speak for themselves, so let them. You just be yourself. There is only one of you and you are unique.

ROLE OF PEACEKEEPER

Everyone experiences a few peace-breaking moments in their families. Living in families where there has been a lot of broken peace can move someone more quickly into the role of peacemaker. A peacemaker jumps quickly into the middle of a situation to try and restore and maintain peace between everyone.

If you identify with this role then which of the following best describes you?

(a) You try to maintain order and calm in every situation at any cost.
(b) You pretend to everyone, for the sake of maintaining peace, that you are OK with the situation.

The problem with (a) is that it is impossible. No matter how hard you work at this, you will just end up exhausted and tense. The problem with (b) is that you are not being honest with yourself or with those around you. (Chapter 4 has tips on dealing with expressing difficult things.)

United Nations peacekeepers play an important role in today's world. They don't ignore difficult situations. Instead, they go into the situation and:

- Listen to different perspectives.
- Work at understanding the circumstances and the differences.
- Over a period of time they negotiate a way forward. Compromises will be needed on both sides.

Be careful that your role of peacemaking in your family is not actually peace-faking.

'When I stopped trying to keep the peace and mind everyone I realised that they were all OK without me. I felt a bit left out as to what role there was for me in the family after that.' DAN (15)

WARNINGS ABOUT ROLE PLAYING

- Sometimes you will find that you have got so caught up in your 'role' that you lose sight of yourself and who you really are. It is important to learn to be yourself.
- Your family is unique and so are you. You are valued in your family for who you are and not for what role you play.
- Take time to develop your own interests so that you can become all that you were created to be.
- It's good to talk to your brothers and sisters too. They are going through the same things as you and you can help each other avoid taking on roles in the family that don't 'fit'.

TIPS ABOUT PARENTS

- Your parents will always be your parents.
- Just because one parent is not living with you in the same house does not mean that he or she will be forgotten.
- A parent does not become less important simply by not living in the same house as you.
- A parent does not become less important because conversation about them with your other parent is more difficult.

- A parent does not get forgotten – ever.
- Tell your parents the things you do appreciate about them. Parents need encouragement too.

New Partners and New Babies

Adjusting to life after your parents' separation takes time. Yet, often long before you feel you have had enough time to adjust to your parents' relationship ending, you may find yourself being introduced to a parent's new partner. If such new relationships contributed to the end of your parents' marriage, this will make it more difficult for you initially.

> 'When Dad decided to remarry I was disappointed as well as angry. He and Mum had been separated for five years, but I guess I had always hoped and dreamed of them getting back together again. When he remarried, I realised this was never going to happen.' AISLING (16)

FANTASY OVER

Even though your parents may have been separated for a long time, it is not until you see them with new partners that you begin to accept their marriage is really over. People often carry the fantasy of parents 'getting-back-together-and-living-happily-ever-after' from childhood into their teen years. Letting go of this can be difficult, but it is important to come to terms with and accept that the relationship has ended. Your parents will, over time, adjust and move on with their lives, and it is important to them that you can do the same. Moving on with your life is about coming to terms with how your family is now. It is about learning to live in the present and look to the future. Moving on is about taking one step at a time; it is not about becoming detached from your family. Your parents will always be your parents. Separation does not end their relationship with you, just with each other.

ADJUSTMENTS FOR PARENTS

There are a lot of adjustments parents have to make in their own lives that you might not think of, since their adjustments will be different to yours. A few of these are:

- Not being with their children 24/7 in the way they have been used to.
- Having sole rather than shared responsibility for children for periods of time.
- Having time to spend alone.
- Being a single person again.
- Financial adjustments.

During this difficult period of readjustment, some parents will find themselves forming a new relationship.

NEW RELATIONSHIPS

Your parent feels that this is a chance for a new start in his or her life – you think the opposite. Your parent thinks that a new relationship will bring positive changes for him or her – you see it as negative in relation to you.

> 'I really wanted my mum and dad to be happy apart, but I didn't want them to meet somebody else either.' JOANNA (14)

> 'Mum had an affair and then a few months later Dad was having an affair too. I think they were just trying to get back at each other. It was like we didn't exist or matter in the family. My grandparents were the only ones interested in us. I just felt like I was in the way of my parents' lives.' NIAMH (13)

You would probably prefer some time to pass before having to get to know a new partner in your parent's life, but the reality is often different. Your parent might be ready to start a new relationship, but seldom will you and your parent agree on the timing. At whatever stage your parent decides to go out with other people, you will probably feel uncomfortable and embarrassed. Don't forget that your parent will be feeling anxious and uneasy too. It will take time for you to become comfortable with his or her new partner and for the new partner to get to know you. Sometimes it helps to think of and treat a new partner as if he or she is one of your friend's parents. You do not have to like him or her, but it is important to show respect in the same way that you would wish to be respected.

> 'When we went to stay with Dad, she was just there. He hadn't even told us about her. It was so awkward and I felt really uncomfortable. Dad should have talked to us first.' TIM (13)

Parents often don't know what to say to their children regarding new partners and make the mistake, like Tim's dad, of saying nothing at all.

> 'It has taken me a long time to get used to Mum's boyfriend. It just felt strange at first, seeing her with someone else. Now it's OK. I guess I accept him now and it is good to see her happier.' EMMA (16)

'I liked Dad's girlfriend when I met her. She was really friendly and interested in what I was doing, but didn't interfere between me and Dad. I think my mum found it hard that I liked her. It was easier not to mention her at home to Mum.'
LUKE (14)

A new partner can never take the place of your parent. Don't assume that he or she wants to, and remind your parent of this fact too.

'Don't assume that if we meet someone a few times we will end up getting married. Please give us permission to go out sometimes with other people, without turning it into a "serious" relationship in your head.' A PARENT

A GAME OF CHESS

'When Mum started going out with someone, I found it really difficult. I wasn't sure where I fitted in any more. I felt that I was being pushed into second place.' JIM (14)

If you have ever played a game of chess, you will know that moving one piece on the board has an impact on the other pieces. Before making a move you must stop, look at the board, and work out the next move and how it will affect or influence the whole game.

New people coming into your family life will have an impact. Seeing a parent involved in a new relationship can bring up all sorts of feelings. This is normal. It's important, however, to think about the situation and plan your 'moves', rather than moving yourself impulsively around the 'board'.

Sometimes a 'move' can leave you wondering where you fit in. You may even be wondering if your parent's love for you has changed. It's easy to feel a little jealous because this new person is getting some of the attention that your parent used to just give you. If you are missing having time alone with your parent, then let him or her know this so that you can arrange some time together.

A good question to ask yourself is: 'Why am I against, upset about or afraid of this new relationship?'

Remember that just because your family group is changing does not mean that your original family no longer exists. Your original family will always include the same people. Your parent's love for you does not change by his or her being in a new relationship.

JANE'S STORY

'I was the eldest in the family and, when Mum and Dad separated, Mum would confide in me and ask my opinion on everything. We would discuss and work out things like holidays, weekends and lots of other things. I felt totally bypassed once her new partner came on the scene. It was like my opinion was no longer relevant.' JANE (18)

When Jane's mum started to go out with someone, Jane felt left out and missed the relationship she had had with her mum. Jane's resentment grew and started to spoil her relationship with her mum, her brother and her mum's partner. When Jane spoke with a counsellor in school and asked herself, 'What am I upset about?' she recognised that the issue was not her mum's partner. The issue was that she missed having one-to-one time with her mum, when they could confide in and talk to each other about things.

Jane talked to her mum about what was making her unhappy. She and her mum started to go out for a few hours on their own on a regular basis. Jane found that she was able to get on more easily with everyone at home after she had thought about and talked her problem through.

BABIES

Finding out that a baby is due in your parent's new relationship can come as a surprise or a shock. Whatever your reaction to the news, it can leave you wondering where you fit in. Perhaps you were the youngest and now that place will go to the new baby. Jealousy can often show up when a new baby arrives. It can be hard seeing your parent spending more time with this baby than they are able to spend with you. The reality is that babies do take up a lot of time. In fact, babies are a 24/7 job. Parents get less sleep and become more stressed because of this. It was the same when you were born, so be patient. It is not a stage that will last forever. It is OK to ask your parent for some time alone with him or her if that is what you want, but this may need some planning ahead.

'Mum being pregnant and my dad not being the father was really embarrassing for me. I felt that the baby was just complicating everything and didn't actually belong in my family. It was different after she was born. Somehow having her there made a difference.' **DAMIEN (16)**

'It just doesn't seem fair that this baby has my dad living with her all the time. He spends so much time with the baby. He never had time for me and my brother when we were small. I know I am older now, but it is still hard to accept this.' **JEN (19)**

'I felt pushed out of my family by the new baby.' **ALICE (12)**

'I hated when Dad's girlfriend was pregnant, but it was better after the baby was born. I liked that I was not an only child any more. The hardest thing for me was that I felt bad for Mum. I think it was harder for her, but there wasn't really anything I could do to change things. I felt a bit guilty about wanting to be at Dad's house a lot.' **JEANNETTE (14)**

'I made a decision that I would have nothing to do with this baby. I switched off and completely ignored its existence. I have told nobody about him because I am too embarrassed and angry. I know he's my half-brother but, as far as I am concerned, he doesn't exist in my life. I know my attitude makes my dad angry and it means I don't spend much time with him. I miss that.' NUALA (15)

'I was afraid that we wouldn't get to see Dad as much because of the baby. It was a bit weird at the start, as we all had to keep quiet in the house. He's three years old now and I love him to bits, but I still feel a bit jealous that he has my dad all of the time.' LAURA (16)

LIFE GOES ON

You may welcome a new baby into your wider family with great excitement or with lots of questions and concerns about how things will work out. Take a few minutes to think about the fact that:

- This baby is related to you.
- This baby is your half-brother or half-sister.
- This baby is innocent – he or she has had no part to play in the family or situation that it has arrived into.

It may seem easier or less painful to cut yourself off from this baby. In the future (which may not seem very relevant to you today), you may regret not having given yourself the opportunity to be an older sister or brother, and your younger sibling will haved missed out on you being a positive part of his or her life. If this sounds over-the-top, just remember that the choices you make for yourself at this time can have long-term consequences. Be careful that you do not make decisions too hastily at a time when you are in a bit of an emotional crisis. It is important to keep contact with both your parents, difficult as it may be. Keep all your options open. You may regret not doing so in the future.

TIPS FOR DEALING WITH YOUR PARENTS' NEW RELATIONSHIPS

- It will take time to adjust to the fact that a new partner is in your parent's life.
- Remember that your other parent is not being replaced.
- A new partner does not want to take the place of your other parent.
- Getting along with a new partner does not mean that you get along with your other parent less.
- Try not to compare your mother to your father's girlfriend.
- Try not to compare your father to your mother's boyfriend.
- Speak respectfully – talk to new partners as you would speak to the parent of one of your friends.
- You do not have to like a new partner, but make sure you treat him or her as you would want to be treated.
- See him or her as another adult who is looking out for you.
- It will take time to adjust to it not being just you and your parent at home.
- If you feel that you want some one-to-one time with your parent, then ask for it. It is OK to ask.

Families Joining Together

WHAT IS A NORMAL FAMILY?

Somehow it seems that, after their parents separate, people start to believe that they are no longer part of a 'normal' family. Families are complicated. If you are now living with a group of people that includes a parent's new partner and his or her children, it can be hard to decide what normal actually is, as you work together to establish a new routine.

If you are living between two homes and two parents then, according to statistics, you are still living in a normal family environment. Normal means 'typical' and 'average'. If you believe that your family is 'abnormal' or 'odd' then it will be more difficult for you to live positively within it.

When second families start joining together there is no hiding that family life can become complicated and baffling at times. A lot of time, openness and give-and-take is needed because everyday things can suddenly feel strange. Being part of any normal family involves disagreements and arguments. Remember, it is not the absence of disagreements that will make your home happier, but rather learning how to talk things through together. When two families join together, the need for each family member to look at things from the other family member's point of view becomes more important. Learning to listen and allowing differing opinions in a family will make you stronger.

A family that is formed when one of your parents remarries is called a stepfamily. In Ireland, you are more likely to find yourself living in a family where one parent is in a second relationship but has not remarried. (The legal grounds for divorce in Ireland are stricter than in many other countries. They require that a couple must have lived apart for at least four out of the previous five years.) Practical issues of learning to adjust to living with new people who you have only known for a short time will have more of an impact on you than the legal issues of divorce or separation.

SO WHAT DO WE CALL OURSELVES?

What people call their newly formed extended family can become an unnecessary problem. It is really up to you to decide what you are comfortable with. You will find a few ideas here, but you will also see that one name can mean different things to different people.

It's a good idea to talk about this with the rest of the family. Work out what you are each comfortable with, and how you want to be introduced or how you might introduce each other when you are out somewhere and meet people.

> 'I don't really call them anything. I just say Mum's house or Dad's house without referring to anyone in each place.' DAVE (13)

> 'We all get on really well now as a wider, bigger family group. We just call ourselves "The Bunch" – it sounds more fun and feels better than calling ourselves "stepfamily".' LYDIA (20)

'I know it may be silly but I just don't ever call my family my "stepfamily". I hate that name. It makes me feel that I have second best.' SIOBHÁN (16)

'I don't use the name "stepparent" or "stepfamily" because it just makes me think of childish stories. I don't think it really influences me, but I think other people assume it is awful from the start.' MAEVE (14)

BLENDED FAMILY

> 'Blended' is a term used to describe families that contain different family groups.
> A blended family describes a mixing and merging together of different family members and others in order to live together as more of a unit.

'I like that name for my family – it sounds better than "stepfamily", more like we all get on. And we do now.' SHANNON (19)

'"Blended family" is a good name. Bit like a smoothie maker with everyone thrown in and mixed up together. Somehow it doesn't quite taste right to me.'
ELAINE (16)

'I never really got hung up on what to call all these people who had dropped into my life without my choosing. Sorting out what we actually called each other was more important. Calling Dad's partner by her Christian name and agreeing that I would introduce her as Dad's partner and she would introduce me as Dad's son – those things helped me. The big picture mattered less.' COLIN (17)

LINK FAMILY

Some people have used the term 'link family' to 'name' their family. It implies being associated with and connected to each other, i.e. being linked together rather than joined together.

Whatever name you decide on for the group of people that you are living with as a family, two ingredients you will need are openness and honesty.

LEARNING TO LIVE TOGETHER

> *Living together is going to involve making an effort*
> *– on everyone's part.*
> *Relationships take work on both sides.*

DIFFERENT RULES

Your parents are different people. They have different personalities and different characters. The saying that 'opposites attract' is often true. Now that they have separated, and you find yourself living with each of them at different times, you will see these differences more clearly. Each of them will have different attitudes and rules that apply in their own houses. Just because they are both your parents does not mean that their rules will automatically be the same.

It's important not to play one parent off against the other – that will just make life worse for you and for them. If parents are communicating well together, then they may have worked out some of the rules together, which would then be similar. However, when parents are unable to communicate easily with each other, it is the difference in rules that creates the most tension. Problems arise over how late you stay up or stay out, what DVD is suitable (age cert.) and even what food is healthy. The more tension that exists between your parents, the more likely that differing rules will create further discord. Parents can compete with each other as to who is the better parent. If you find this happening then let your parents know that it is not much fun for you living this way. Accepting that your parents are different and learning to adapt to different rules will help everybody.

READ BOTH WAYS

In different situations you learn and apply the appropriate rules. In a library the rules are that you do not talk loudly and you move quietly around the building. In a sports stadium you can scream loudly from where you are standing and no one will be concerned. You have to apply different rules cycling along a road than to mountain biking. Living between two homes with two different sets of rules is possible. You will agree with some and disagree with others. What is important is working out some of the rules with each parent. Compare 'house rules' with a group of your friends and you will discover that their homes will all have different rules too.

Don't fall into the trap of thinking that the grass is always greener on the other side. In other words, be careful not to think that just because you have had an argument with one parent on some issue, your other parent is going to be more understanding.

Parents' new partners are adults with different rules and attitudes who come to share your life and your living space. Working out house rules in these situations brings an even greater need for open communication between you all. Deciding on house rules together is a good idea because then everyone knows what is expected of them. Knowing what is expected makes it easier. Not having things clarified just causes confusion. Suggest getting together and working out a list of house rules whereby everyone has the opportunity to be heard and understood on some of the areas that are important to them. Everyone needs to try and cooperate with each other rather than just competing with each other about whose family rules or traditions are right or wrong.

SPACE

Moving house or moving new people into your house automatically changes things. Having no personal space or a bedroom to call your own is hard to cope with. Privacy may be important to you, so learning to share a room or space that was previously your own is not easy. Having a small space or corner or a few drawers or shelves to yourself can make a difference. Being clear about the rules for respecting each other's property and talking about the importance of privacy is always best done at the start of a new situation, rather than being silent and waiting for matters to explode.

If you spend weekends or shorter times in one home then try and find a way to make this place feel more like your own home too. Ask if you can put a poster on the wall or have a shelf where you can leave your things from one time to the next. Keep a few spare clothes around. Having some of your bits and pieces around will help you feel that you are not just a visitor.

Blending different families doesn't happen easily. The two families will have grown up with different rules, attitudes and different life experiences. You will think differently, believe differently and behave differently. Your sense of humour may not be similar; your interests may be different. These differences are not reasons to judge or decide that this new extended family contains people you will not and cannot get on with.

Take time to get to know them and let them get to know you too. Do not judge too quickly. In spite of the fact that linked families are complicated and difficult, it is still possible for you and this bigger family to become a very strong family unit. A new partner is obviously not your biological parent. If, however, a partner is living in the same house as you, it is important that he or she has a certain amount of authority if he or she is to care about you. It is not easy for the new partner either, so be prepared to consider his or her point of view too.

Living together with anyone will have its frustrations and irritations. Try and take a mental step back from some of the smaller irritations and see if you can learn not to react to them in such a strong manner. Most days, either in school or at home, we all face the reality that not everything is the way we want it to be. Saving some energy for putting into things we enjoy, rather than using it up reacting to every small irritation, is a good life lesson to start practising. When something important needs to be dealt with, you are more likely to be listened to when you have not made issues out of all the small 'stuff'.

BE ORGANISED

These two words can make a big difference to your life running more easily, especially when it involves going to and fro between two homes. Put up a timetable in your room or in your school bag. This will help you plan and remember what is going on in school and after school each day. Do not rely on your parents to remember and remind you of what you need. Plan ahead.

> *Being organised is something you can learn to do for yourself.*
> *Being organised will make things better for you.*

TIME

It takes a long time for people who have moved in together to feel comfortable living as a family. Adjusting to all the changes is a slow process. Learn to take things very slowly. Everyone will have to learn to think carefully before they act.

REALISTIC V. UNREALISTIC EXPECTATIONS

A parent moving in with a new partner and his or her children will often have unrealistic expectations, for instance, that everyone will get on really well without any major problems. Having experienced some difficult relationships in the past, they will be trying to make sure that this new relationship will be a positive and loving one for everyone – that includes you.

It's unrealistic to think that everyone will automatically or, even in time, love each other. That may or may not happen, but what is important is that everyone learns to accept and show respect towards each other. Talking about what is realistic and what people's expectations are is good for the whole family to do together. You might need to suggest it.

RESOLVING ISSUES

We all know the best solutions to problems – usually we think our own solution is the best one. When it comes to resolving issues, make sure you look for different options and choices rather than one answer only. Listening is an important part of finding solutions. In Chapter 4 there are tips to help you work through areas of conflict with others.

ACTION PLAN ...

... for issues that are causing problems at the moment:

- **A**   **A**cknowledge that there is a problem.
- **C**   **C**all a family meeting (anyone in the family is free to call one).
- **T**   **T**hink **T**ank – brainstorm ideas for solutions together.
- **I**   '**I**' not 'U' statements – 'I would like ...' rather than 'You should ...'
- **O**   **O**pinions differ – everyone is entitled to one.
- **N**   **N**egotiate and **N**ame the action that you agree together to put in place and begin to resolve the problem.

Special Occasions

After your parents separate, one thing you will discover is that family celebrations and special occasions (birthdays, Christmas, Confirmation, First Communion, etc.) are some of the most difficult times to deal with. The first birthday or Christmas that you spend without one parent is always the hardest, but, as the years go on, you will find that you all become more comfortable and will even find new and different ways of celebrating together.

Special occasions may trigger unresolved issues and tensions between your parents. This is something you can't control completely. Instead of enjoying some of the excitement, you might start feeling a knot in your stomach that can quickly grow into a ball of anxiety. Special occasions are even more difficult when parents are not on speaking terms.

Other events, such as school PTA meetings, school plays, matches, prize-giving ceremonies or possibly graduation from school, also create anxiety. The anxiety is usually about both parents wanting to be in the same place at the same time and with you. It is also about not knowing how they might behave towards each other, especially in front of your friends or other people.

PLAN AHEAD
SEÁN'S STORY

'My parents are like two different chemicals. Both are great on their own. But put the two test tubes and the two chemicals in the same room, and I am always afraid about the reaction between them and what the result will be. I have seen some unreal chemical explosions.' SEÁN (14)

When he was with them on their own, Seán got on very well with both his parents. However, putting them in the same room was, as far as Seán was concerned, a disaster waiting to happen. He never felt confident about how they would react to each other and he worried about them turning up at school for a PTA meeting or a match at the same time.

The best way to sort out a knotted-up ball of string is to undo the knots. In the same way, the best way of dealing with your anxiety is to unravel it and work out what the main cause of it is.

Seán had a match coming up in school. It was a semi-final and both parents wanted to be there. Seán wanted to be able to concentrate on the match and not have to worry about his parents on the sideline.
His concerns were:

- Will they be rude to each other?
- Will they embarrass me in public and in front of my friends?
- Will I be able to concentrate on my game?
- If my brother is going with my dad, then how will Mum manage being on her own?

People waste a lot of energy worrying about situations and yet nobody seems to talk about them. Everybody has concerns about getting through difficult situations, but, without a plan in place, everybody just keeps carrying the tension around, and it grows.

Working out some ideas and planning a few things ahead of time is worthwhile. If you can decide a plan together with your parents, then you will feel more prepared and in control of the situation.

Seán asked his mum who she was going to the match with. When she replied that she was going on her own, Seán suggested that she bring his aunt with her. He explained that he would like her to have company and that she would have support if they bumped into his dad. Seán also asked his dad if he and Seán's younger brother would sit in the middle so that he would know where they were. Seán explained that it would help him to stay focused on the game and he would also know where to see his dad. His mum knew that Seán's brother and dad were arriving early and where they would be sitting. She arrived just as the match was starting and sat somewhere different. Seán had the courage to tell his parents that this plan would help him to stay focused during the game and they each wanted to support him in making sure that happened.

This might sound very complicated, but this was one occasion shortly after Seán's parents had separated when there was a lot of hostility between them. With time, things improved but, for this occasion, having a plan that was talked out with both of his parents helped Seán to keep his focus on the game and enjoy the occasion.

WORK OUT A PLAN TOGETHER

'My brother's confirmation was the next weekend and none of us knew what was going to happen or what the plan was – or even if there was a plan. We wanted to know if Dad had been invited, would he come anyway, how Mum would react and would Grandad come if he knew Dad was going to be there. No one asked my brother what he wanted. It was all about my parents, even though it should have been all about my brother.' SINÉAD (15)

A plan is the best tool for managing special occasions.

Accept that making a plan will involve some compromises on everyone's part. Make sure that you have been honest and have added your ideas into the planning as well. It is not always easy for your parents either. They will be working some things out as they go along, so your thoughts are helpful. If you have ideas then talk them through. 'Around-the-table discussion':

- Make it open to everyone who is involved.
- Be honest.
- Be creative with ideas and solutions.
- Be willing to compromise on some things.

You will feel more prepared and in control if you have talked about and thought through some of the details. *Make a plan.* Write it down. Let people know what the plan is and what is expected of them.
Some of the plan details might be:

- The time the occasion starts or that your parents are due to arrive at the same place.
- The time the occasion finishes at.
- If there is a meal or food involved, then what will the seating arrangements be? It can be very helpful to have this planned out and spoken openly about. Then everyone will be more comfortable on the day knowing exactly who they will be sitting beside and

- where they are to go. Even if it is an informal setting for food, you can still plan some of these details.
- If you want photographs taken, you can always ask for a photo of you with both of your parents, but it is better to make this wish known ahead of time. If it is not possible, then make sure you get pictures taken with each parent.
- You may have a good friend or a relation that you would like to have with you on the day for support. This is a good idea but do remember to ask for them to be included ahead of time.
- If a parent is struggling with the idea of being together again for the occasion, encourage him or her to include a relation or friend who can give support. If your parents are uncomfortable speaking to each other, accept this. Do not try and force the issue.
- Confirmations are occasions when you could join with another person from your confirmation group and his or her family to go for a meal together. More people and two different families can dilute some of the tension.
- Work at making the occasion enjoyable.

CHRISTMAS AND EASTER

There are times in the year when you may find it impossible to keep both parents happy. Accepting this will help you to focus on what *is* possible, and also on what is *not* possible.

Trying to divide your time up, and considering both parents, is the best thing you can do. Obviously, if you live further away from each other then the holiday times can be an opportunity to spend time with the parent you see least of. Some parents plan a calendar over two years, which can mean that you spend Christmas Day this year with one parent and Christmas Day of the following year with the other.

> *'Both my parents want me to please them by agreeing to do things their way. It puts me in a battle that I can never win.'* JANET (16)

Sometimes parents lose sight of just how important your other parent is in your life, especially when it comes to having to juggle holiday times. You will, over time, learn to adjust and divide your time between the two different homes and worlds of both your parents.

> *Trying to arrange to see your parents can be a pain but remember that what matters is that everyone does want to, and is trying to, make time for each other. It may not always be easy to sort out, but it is worth it.*

TRIPLE-DECKER SANDWICH

Christmas and special occasions are times when everyone, including parents, grandparents, relatives and cousins on both sides of the family, wants to spend time with you. Add the further ingredients of relations of your parents' new partners (if they have them) and you can find yourself sandwiched in the middle of a large number of people. Your parents will be getting pulled in a lot of directions at these times too. You will not be able to please them all. But keeping things in perspective and being willing to offer your ideas on how to make certain occasions at least tolerable will help.

OLD AND NEW TRADITIONS

Certain times of the year will have different associations and traditions for you. Traditions are important, but don't miss the opportunity to create new traditions too. Traditionally, in my home, we have always had a real Christmas tree, usually dragged in through the back door. However, if I went to live on the sixth floor of a building with limited space, then I would change to a small artificial tree. I might miss the smell of pine, but I could get used to it and enjoy having a tree anyway. Alternatively, I could stay angry and resent the change and decide that Christmas is spoiled because things are not the way they have always been.

Making the best of each day at these times of the year depends a lot on your own attitude. It is very difficult to make changes and lose some traditions that have been important to you for many years. It may be that you will be able to keep some of them and change others as you all adapt to different ideas. Only seeing what is wrong or different and staying bitter and resentful will stop you enjoying the occasion. Being able to talk about the things you miss will help. Remember that you have all your memories from your past to this point. They are part of your story and who you are, and will always be there. This year, add new good memories to your life story. Don't stop adding and making new ones – they are important too.

> *Accepting where you are today does not mean forgetting your family history and your own life story.*

Things will always change. It is part of life. It takes time to adjust to and live with family changes, but it is also important to make the most of your family the way it is now.

TRIGGERS FROM THE PAST

> '*I still find that there are occasions when I see my parents together and it triggers old emotions. They are still the two most important people in my life and it is hard accepting that they don't get on well enough to live together.*' JANE (18)

There will always be times when you will get a little knocked off balance by your emotions. Sometimes you will see it coming and other times it just may be that you hear a song, see a photo or get asked a question that triggers something from the past.

Special occasions often remind us of how things used to be and how much things have changed. It takes effort and willingness to cooperate when things are not the same or are not how you want them to be. It can be good to talk about some of these nostalgic moments with someone who will understand that there are occasions that leave you feeling sad at what has changed. This can happen for many years after parents separate. The best thing to do at these times is to talk about it.

Difficult Situations

'It took a long time for me to stop turning my parents' problems into my own problems. It was hard not to get involved.' SHANNON (19)

'I would put my headphones on and play my music loudly and try and block out the yelling. I was too frightened to go out of my room, but I was also really scared of what might happen if I just stayed there too. I never knew what to do. I never knew what was going to happen and I was too afraid to tell anyone what was going on.' MARTIN (16)

'I think Dad wanted to believe we were all OK, but I think he was too afraid to ask us.' EMILY (17)

'It was a strange feeling when I realised that, if my parents couldn't help themselves, then they couldn't help me either.' GERRY (17)

'There was an unspoken pact that no one talked about Mum's drinking. I just felt that I ended up having to deal with a lot of my parents' problems because neither of them would deal with them themselves.' SUE (16)

The fact that your parents have separated is difficult enough without adding any extra stress factors. If your parents' problems include issues such as alcoholism, violence, drug or other addictions, or a serious mental health problem, then this will make your life even more complicated. No one can protect or immunise you from the pain these circumstances create. You may feel completely alone in coping, but it is important to know that there are people who have lived with and understand the situation that you are in.

Secrecy often plays a big role in a family dealing with uncomfortable issues. But, in the end, secrecy does not help you. Secrecy can end up supporting the 'problem' rather than helping you or your family to get support. How our family appears to everyone else can be very different to how we know our family actually lives. Your parent may be well respected in his or her community and workplace and yet, at home, behave in totally unacceptable ways to you. There are many useful websites and telephone numbers for support services and agencies at the end of this book. Pick up the phone and talk to someone today. You will get support and reassurance from the information and advice they can give you.

THE '3 C RULE'

You will have probably spent hours trying to work out how you can change the situation at home. No matter what is going on in the lives of your parents, it is important to accept and apply the '3 C Rule' to your own situation.

> **Important – Remember the '3 C Rule':**
>
> *You can't CAUSE someone to behave in a particular way (e.g. to drink).*
>
> *You can't CURE someone of a particular illness or behaviour.*
>
> *You can't CHANGE someone – this is only something they can do for themselves.*

There are always going to be things about your parents' relationship that you will not know about or understand. It can be easy to blame the parent who is the alcoholic or who would appear to have the most difficult personality for the marriage or relationship ending. However, usually other problems would have occurred in the relationship that you would know nothing about. Taking sides and blaming one of your parents won't help you. Each of your parents will often, either subtly or clearly, try and get you on his or her 'side' and feel justified in telling you lots of information when, in fact, it would be better for you to be allowed to step back from the issues that are mainly theirs to work out.

In many cases, one parent will stay in a difficult relationship because of the belief that he or she can help the other person to change. It takes a long time to realise that this isn't possible. People themselves must take responsibility for making changes to their own lives.

If you are living in a difficult home situation at the moment, you don't need a book to tell you that everyone in the family is suffering at some level. You need to know that it is not OK for you to be living your own life feeling unhappy and negative all the time. It is important to tell someone what is going on. Talk to an adult you can trust. Remember that it is your parents' behaviour that is unacceptable to you. The unacceptable behaviour hides their good qualities, which you also know. This is why it is so difficult and confusing to deal with.

HOW STRESS AFFECTS YOU

Living with tension at home all the time and not knowing how each day will turn out can lead to stress. Stress can make you lose concentration in school or at other times, and leave you unable to sleep. You may feel unwell a lot of the time.

Stress can make you feel:
- Confused.
- Powerless in a situation.
- Protective of a parent.
- Resentful towards a parent.
- Ashamed.
- Guilty at not being able to stop or control a situation.
- Protective towards younger siblings.
- Extra responsibility.

Bottling up all these feelings will make you feel worse. Talking to someone who understands your circumstances will help. Whatever your worries, there is help available for you and your family. Look at the list of the support services and helplines in Appendix 2 and pick up the phone or go online now.

HOW STRESS AFFECTS YOUR FRIENDSHIPS

If you hide behind your parents' problems, it will stop other people from getting to know *you*.

The secrecy and shame that can surround a family can make it difficult to develop friendships in school. You may not want to bring people home because you don't know how things will be when you get there. It is important that you have a friend who knows and understands the situation so that you have his or her support. Friends can be a lifeline.

Find ways of dealing with your anger or bitterness that do not damage your friendships with others. Don't take out your frustrations on your friends.

CRISIS PLAN

Being prepared for a crisis at home will give you a greater sense of control. It is like knowing the fire drill in school and where to go and what to do in an emergency. When you understand the drill you can put it into practice when the warning bell rings.

- Have an arrangement with a friend or a relative who is not living with you so that, for instance, if you phone them and use a code

word, then they will understand the importance or urgency of a situation without you having to explain everything at that moment.
- Put this number in your mobile phone or write it down and put it close to the phone at home.
- Arrange with this person that you can go to his or her home at any time – if he or she will give you a spare key then that might be helpful (or know where it is hidden).
- Involve your parent in this plan if possible.
- If you are under 18, in the eyes of the law you are still a child and have rights that protect you. Family services (e.g. social workers) are there to support families through a crisis and want to work with your family, not against them.
- While you may feel responsible and old enough to deal with the situations you find yourself in, it is often not appropriate. Your parents are the adults and are responsible for you (not the reverse).

THE RIGHT TO BE SAFE

Under the Irish Constitution and also under the United Nations Convention on the Rights of the Child (again, a child is anyone under the age of 18) you have the right to live in safety and without fear of being harmed. You have the right to be safe and protected from any kind of physical, sexual or emotional abuse. This is true no matter who is looking after you. It is important for you to know that there are laws to protect children and provide proper care when parents fail in their responsibility to do so.

The only way to get away from abuse is to tell someone. If you have any worries about your safety, please tell an adult who you can trust or contact one of the organisations listed in Appendix 2.

ALCOHOLISM

If you have a parent who misuses or abuses alcohol, then it is important to take on board the '3 C Rule':

> You cannot **cause** your parent to drink.
> You cannot **cure** his or her drinking.
> Much as you may want to, you cannot **change** his or her drinking behaviour.

Alcoholism is an illness. Only the person with the disease can be treated. Alcoholism creates family problems, but getting involved in trying to control your parent's actions and taking over responsibilities that are not yours will not help anyone in the long term.

Organisations such as Al-anon and Alateen are there to give you and other family members support.

Don't forget to have a **crisis plan** worked out for situations that you might be concerned about finding yourself in, for example, a parent wanting to drive you home after he or she has been drinking.

> **Alcoholism is a disease, not a disgrace.**

'The hardest thing for me to deal with was that there was help there for my mum to get treated for her alcoholism, but she wouldn't take the help.'

HANNAH (16)

'When you live with a parent who is an alcoholic, you just live with constant broken promises. I don't think you ever really get used to that.' LIAM (17)

TIPS FOR DEALING WITH DIFFICULT FAMILY SITUATIONS

- Stay in contact with your friends and spend time with them.
- Don't ignore the problem.
- Trust and tell a friend about the situation at home. It is good to have an adult to talk to as well, e.g. an aunt, uncle, grandparent, or someone in school or your youth group who will understand and support you at home. Talking about your worries stops them from building up.
- If your parent suffers from mental health issues (e.g. severe depression) then get lots of information on the illness. Alcoholism is also an illness and it is good to get information on this, rather than just knowing about its consequences. Facts and information will help you feel you have greater control of the situation.
- Stay involved in activities both inside and outside of school. Having contact with others and enjoying free time will help keep life

positive and stop the 'situation' from taking over. Often it is the 'situation' (e.g. mental illness, alcoholism, addiction, violence) that becomes the whole focus of family life. It is important to keep developing your own interests as well.

- Keep a balance. Doing too much and never stopping can be as unhelpful as doing nothing at all. Look at your own lifestyle and keep a balance between school, work and relaxing.
- You are as important as other family members. Sometimes the situation at home puts all the attention on the one person. Things must be put back into perspective.
- Put a *crisis plan* in place for any situation that you may be feeling anxious about.
- Ask for help. Help is always available and it shows courage, not weakness, to look for it.

11 Advice from Teenagers ...

ADVICE TO PARENTS

What do you wish parents understood about separation from your point of view?

Here you will find many comments from young people in response to this question.

You could use any of their comments as a starting point for talking to your own parents about an issue that is affecting you at the moment. This chapter could also be for parents to read in order for them to understand a little more about life from a young person's perspective, during and after parental separation.

TALK TO US

'Please don't assume that you know what is good for your children without even stopping and talking to them, and hearing their opinions.'

'Don't assume that we are OK, even if we say that we are. How can we be OK when everything has changed and is a mess and nothing is actually OK anymore?'

'Find out what your children are thinking. Why should they care about what you think if you don't care enough to find out about what they think?'

'Don't assume that you know and understand how your children feel about something when you haven't asked them and they haven't told you.'

'Parents should not expect their children to fit in with their schedule, without first talking about it with them.'

'Even though you don't talk to us about what is going on, this does not mean we are not aware of it. When the house is full of different moods between us all, it is difficult to manage.'

'It is really frustrating when you pretend that everything and everyone is all right and nobody talks about anything at all.'

'Don't tell your children that everything is going to be the same and OK. You might want to believe it, but it is a lie.'

COMMUNICATE WITH EACH OTHER

'Please find a way to keep in touch with each other and communicate about us without using us as your messengers.'

'It is really difficult for us when you refuse to talk to each other. We know there are reasons, but we wish that you could sometimes talk about us, as parents, and leave the other things aside for a while.'

'When you give us a message to pass on, it means we get all the person's emotion and reaction to the message, if it's something they don't want to hear. This is not fair and is really upsetting.'

'Sometimes it is like you are competing against each other to be the best and most responsible parent. There's no fun being in a family like this.'

'Please don't use us to play your games between each other. We wish that you could both be on the side of the family.'

WHAT YOU TELL US

'If you are going to give us important information, please try and give it to us together so that there are no wires crossed and everyone hears the same thing.'

'As parents, you each expect us to trust what you tell us. If you each give different messages, then we end up trusting neither of you.'

'Sometimes parents try to make things easier for us by telling us half truths. In the end, we prefer honesty.'

'The only details I ever got about my parents' divorce were about money and financial things. Those details made things worse. Parents should think carefully about what details they give their children.'

WHAT YOU SAY ABOUT EACH OTHER

'Please don't criticise my other parent in front of me. I hate it when you both do that. Genetically, I am 50 per cent of each of you. When you rubbish each other, it feels like you are rubbishing part of me.'

'If I do something that you don't like, then I always hear, "You're just like your mother" or "You got that habit from your father." Sometimes it is as though I only hear what's wrong with me from both of you.'

'Don't ever tell your children that everyone would be better off if the other parent was dead. Even though one parent is not living at home, at least they still have both their parents.'

TIME WITH US

'It is hard for us to work out how to have a relationship with a parent who is not living at home. You need to show us.'

'It is important that we have some time on our own with you and not just always all of us children together. Usually we spend Wednesdays with Dad, but sometimes I would like it to be just me and him.'

'Parents should make time for their children. Especially in the beginning, they should make an effort and pick up their children rather than expecting the kids to get to them. When parents do this, it makes their children feel that they really want to see them, rather than it just being an arrangement parents have to keep to.'

'If there has been a gap in time between you and your kids talking to each another, then you should remember that they have probably changed because of the experience too, and things aren't the same as when you spoke to them last.'

'When parents [non-resident] spend time with their children, they need to try a bit harder to have a good time. When I see my dad he always seems down and talks of missing me, and I feel guilty. I have to keep telling myself that it's not my fault and I don't need to feel guilty. I wish he could just enjoy being with me a bit more when we are together.'

'When you are with us, you are not babysitting. You are being our parent. Don't make us feel like we are just a babysitting job to you.'

'Time with your parent is what you need to build a relationship. Time is what is valuable. Looking back, that is what was missing and now it is so much harder.'

'If you want a relationship with your child, just show them love and make an effort.'

'It's little things that make good memories. We might benefit from both of you wanting to get us stuff, but it is the little things that you do with us that mean the most.'

'The weird thing about my family was that, before they separated, my parents were always busy and away and didn't want me around. Now that they've separated, they both keep fussing and wanting to "make time". I think what I feel most sad about is that my family separated before I ever had the experience of living as a family the way I thought a family would.'

'I wish Dad knew how much I miss him, but what makes me saddest is that, even if he knew, I don't think it would make any difference.'

'Please remember that, as we get older, our plans at weekends change too. We still want to spend time with you, but we also don't want to miss out on a party. Please be prepared to be flexible and understand this.'

'If your plans change for seeing me, then please give me the option of a different time to meet. Don't just cancel.'

THERE ARE SOME THINGS WE NEED YOU, AS PARENTS, TO UNDERSTAND

'Give us time to be OK with all the changes. Don't expect us to accept things as quickly as you might want us to.'

'Don't expect us to accept new relationships in your life straight away. Our love is for both our parents.'

'Try and remember that we have to deal with everything as well. We are not immune to the situation.'

'Be careful of and more aware of not dumping all your "emotional stuff" on us at home. Find support somewhere else and let us be neutral.'

'Just because we keep doing things that we need to do, like school, clubs, college, seeing our friends, doesn't mean that everything is OK.'

'Sometimes it feels like we are all going round in circles on an emotional rollercoaster. We realise that it is the same for you, but we need you to understand that it is the same for us too.'

MORE THINGS WE NEED YOU TO UNDERSTAND

'You may have separated years ago, but there are still times when I get really upset and it is still difficult.'

'We worry too and wonder about what's going to happen next.'

'Sometimes you need to put what you want on hold and find out what your children want, especially about things that are happening in our lives, like school.'

'As parents you were always just there ... now I have to plan my life and diary around seeing you and trying to keep you both happy by balancing my time. I love you both, but it's a pain.'

ADVICE TO OTHER TEENAGERS

'Remember – it's not your fault.'

'Trying to arrange times to see your parents can be a pain, but remember that what matters is that everyone wants to, and is trying to, make time for each other. It's not easy but it is worth it.'

'No matter how much you think about your parents separating and your family, you can't actually change the fact or control it.'

'Try not to get involved in everything that is going on at home. Work at trying to keep the focus on your own life and school, friends, sport, college, etc.'

'Remember who the parent is and who the child is. Don't be your parent's parent. Find a neutral person to talk to.'

'Keeping things bottled up makes you unhappy.'

'Learn to recognise what is appropriate and inappropriate about what you are being told by either parent. You don't have to sit and listen and take anything that makes you feel uncomfortable. You have the right to leave a situation, discussion or argument, but do this in a respectful way to yourself and the other person.'

'Let your parents know what you are feeling. It helps sort some things out if there is interaction between you and your parents, rather than you trying to sort it all out in your head.'

'Suggest that your parents ask you, "Do you want to talk?" rather than them just saying, "What's wrong?"'

'Get a diary for yourself and write down the schedule. Talk through your own plans ahead of time as much as you can with your parents, so that there may be time to change things if possible.'

'There isn't just one way of doing things and all kinds of living arrangements are possible.'

'Parents separating complicates life but, over time, you will find ways of managing your new family situation.'

Last Word 12

When parents separate, it is bound to cause you pain. If they can manage to work through parenting and other issues together, this can lessen that pain. Many parents, however, get caught on the emotional roller-coaster caused by separation. You may have a hard job avoiding being caught in the middle of the two people who mean so much to you.

Moving through your teenage years towards independent adulthood will present plenty of challenges. Be honest with yourself in some of the more difficult situations. If you walk around with your shoe-laces untied you are likely to trip up. If your attitude is that nothing will ever be quite right because your parents have separated, you will miss out on so much. It is possible, though not always easy, to stop and tie the laces on your own shoes. That means learning how to live with your new circumstances and move into all that is ahead for you. Don't waste your life waiting for someone to tie your laces or blaming others for the fact that the laces are undone in the first place. Your attitude will have a huge impact on how you manage.

I have had the privilege of talking to many of you whose parents have separated. I have been impressed by the courage and strength that you have shown in dealing with difficult situations at home and yet still continuing to get on with your own lives in healthy and enjoyable ways. You may know the 'Serenity Prayer':

God grant me the serenity to accept the things I cannot change,
Courage to change the things I can
And wisdom to know the difference.

These words are worth remembering in all situations.

Never hesitate to ask for help. It is always available and it shows courage, not weakness, to look for it. This book can only deal with issues in a general way. In doing so, I would never wish to play down your own situation.

Live your life positively. Influence your world for good. This might sound like some grand statement that applies to somebody else. But it is your life and your life is important. Please take time, especially in difficult situations, to think about and choose what you will do ... and choose wisely.

APPENDIX 1
Legal Terms

Most parents will want to sort out their problems and the legal issues around their separation without involving their children. The legal process aims to support and encourage parents to work out good agreements between themselves without having to go to court.

When parents are unable to agree on things themselves, it is because they both have different ideas on how best to separate. At these times, a case will come before a judge in a family law court. These cases are always carried out in private. Judges will be very aware of how difficult these times are for a family and will have a very definite and genuine concern for any children involved.

They are bound by the law to make decisions in what they believe to be the best interests of the child. It is important for a judge to have clear information and details about whether children:

- Have access to both parents so that it is possible to maintain a good relationship with each one.
- Live in a safe home where they are cared for.
- Can continue their education with as little interruption as possible.
- Have adequate financial support.

Currently in Ireland, young people are not allowed to be present in the family court for any actual hearings. This is primarily to protect them. Judges are anxious that teenagers are not put in the position of having to take sides or that one parent doesn't influence or control a teenager's comments.

As time goes on, your views and opinions can change. Some of the details of separation agreements can be renegotiated at different times in the future to accommodate situations changing and you getting older. Here are some general legal terms you might hear that relate to family separation and divorce.

ACCESS

Access is the contact a parent has with the child he or she is not living with. Access usually involves an agreed arrangement for spending time together. It can also refer to other forms of communication such as phone calls, e-mail and letters. Access agreements and access orders are made through your local District Court, if parents are unable to reach agreements on arrangements themselves. Access orders can also be made in the Circuit Court and High Court when an application is made for a judicial separation or a divorce.

Access is also the right of a child (anyone under age 18). Article 9 of the United Nations Convention on the Rights of the Child states: 'The child has the right to maintain contact with both parents if separated from one or both.' This means that, if one parent no longer lives full time with you, you have the *right* to be able to keep in contact with him or her and have the opportunity to have a good relationship with him or her (providing it is safe for you to do so).

Supervised Access involves having another adult present with you when you have time with a parent. In exceptional circumstances, this is put in place for your protection.

AFFIDAVIT
An affidavit is a written statement that is used in court and which is sworn on oath to be true.

BARRING ORDER
A barring order is a court order that prevents a violent person from remaining to live in the family home. It forbids the person from threatening to use violence and can also ban him or her from watching or being around the area of the family home.

BARRISTER
A barrister is an advocate (one who pleads the cause of another). He or she is usually instructed by the solicitor who is taking the case before the courts.

CHILD
In Ireland this term refers to anyone under the age of 18. A child remains dependent until 18 years of age or 23 years of age, if in full-time education.

COHABITATION
Cohabitation is used to describe an adult relationship where people are living together as a couple (and in a sexual relationship) without being legally married.

COLLABORATIVE LAW
Collaborative law is a method of helping separating couples (with the help of their collaborative lawyers) to resolve disputes and reach agreements on all issues arising, without the need to go to court (except to legalise their agreement). Certain members of the legal profession have trained as collaborative lawyers (see <http://www.acp.ie>).

COUNSELLING
Counselling involves meeting with someone, individually or in a group, who offers direction, support and advice on personal issues. Partaking in marriage counselling and family counselling would provide opportunities to understand and work at resolving differences.

COURT
Court is where judges and solicitors meet to hear legal cases. In Ireland there are Circuit Family Courts where separation and divorce cases are usually dealt with. Sometimes parents can't agree about some of the arrangements and, when this happens, specially trained solicitors and barristers get involved in order to help sort out the situation.

Applications for barring, safety and protection orders, together with applications for guardianship, custody and access, and maintenance are dealt with in the District Court.

COURT ORDER
This is an instruction given by a court or a judge that requires someone to do or not to do something. The Circuit Family Court has the authority to make orders about guardianship, custody and access matters, maintenance, property and other financial issues.

CUSTODY
Custody is the physical day-to-day care and control of a child. In Ireland, the courts have the power to make an order for joint custody so that the child can spend time with each parent, even in cases where primary care is agreed or given to one parent only.

DIVORCE
This is the legal ending of a marriage. In Ireland, a Decree of Divorce can only be granted where the couple has lived apart for four years and where proper provision has been made for the children of the marriage and for both parents. A Decree of Divorce does not affect the legal rights of any child of that marriage. Being divorced allows people to legally remarry, should they wish to do so.

GUARDIANS
Guardians have a right and a responsibility to make sure that a child is properly cared for. They have a part in the decisions that relate to a child's welfare, including educational, health, social, religious and other

decisions. For any children born to married parents, both parents have joint guardianship rights and responsibilities. Guardianship is not the same as custody, although a guardian has the right of custody against all third parties who are not guardians.

GUARDIAN AD LITEM

A *Guardian ad Litem* is an independent professional appointed by the courts in a variety of proceedings concerning children, such as care proceedings and private family law matters. He or she will work to ensure that the welfare and best interests of the child remain the primary consideration throughout proceedings, particularly where matters are contentious, or where important care issues must be decided by the court. The *Guardian ad Litem* will give full consideration to the views and opinions of the child and will act as a voice or advocate for the child in the proceedings.

JUDICIAL SEPARATION

A judicial separation can be granted by the Circuit (Family) Court or the High Court on certain grounds including where there has been no normal marital relationship for a period of one year prior to the application. When the court grants a judicial separation it must consider the needs of both parents and the needs of the children in relation to financial and other resources available to the family. The rights of a child remain unaffected by a judicial separation being given.

MAINTENANCE

Maintenance is the amount of money paid at specified intervals from one parent to another for the care and support of that parent and/or any dependent children of the family.

MEDIATION

Mediation helps couples who have decided to separate to work out their own agreements and decisions together. Mediation will address the needs and interests of children and practical issues. It also helps parents to manage conflict in a way that protects the best interests of their children.

NULLITY/ANNULMENT

In certain cases, a court can decide that a marriage is null and void. A marriage is annulled when it is considered that the marriage did not, in law, exist. In these very limited cases the rights of any children are still protected by many laws, e.g. Guardianship of Infants Act, Family Law Act and Status of Children Act. The relationship between a parent and child is unaffected.

PROTECTION ORDER

A protection order is a temporary legal order that forbids someone from making any threats or carrying out acts of violence, but still allows him or her to stay in the home, pending an application for a safety order.

RESIDENCE/HABITUAL RESIDENCE

Your residence is simply the place where you live. Your country of habitual residence is usually determined by your parents. It is not open to one parent to change your country of residence without the consent of the other parent. Where this occurs, it can result in child abduction proceedings being brought against one parent by the other parent in the High Court.

SAFETY ORDER

A safety order is a legal order that forbids someone from making any threats or acts of violence, but allows him or her to stay in the home. A protection order is similar to a safety order, but is granted for a shorter period of time.

SEPARATION AGREEMENT/DEED OF SEPARATION

This is a legal agreement to live apart made between married couples. Such an agreement is made without making an application to a court. It is very important that both parties obtain independent legal advice before entering into a Deed of Separation.

SETTLEMENT/CONSENT TERMS

A couple can come to an agreement on how to approach the future living separately, each making compromises. This agreement is called a settlement or consent terms when it is lodged in court as part of judicial separation or divorce proceedings. It is normal, and is advised, that each parent gets independent legal advice on these issues.

SOCIAL WORKERS

A social worker is a person who is trained and available to help and support children and families at difficult times and in difficult situations. Social workers make recommendations to the court regarding care arrangements.

SOLICITOR

A solicitor has legal training and will advise people on the legal issues around separation and divorce. He or she will also represent individuals in court proceedings. In separation, each parent will have his or her own solicitor. This is a normal procedure.

APPENDIX 2

Useful Contact Information

ACCORD
(http://www.accord.ie)
Offers safe, professional and confidential support for couples and individuals in their marriages and relationships.
Address: Central Office, Columba Centre, Maynooth, Co. Kildare
Tel.: (01) 5053112
E-mail: admin@accord.ie

AIM FAMILY SERVICES
(http://www.aimfamilyservices.ie)
Offers a confidential family law information service and family mediation service. AIM provides a number of useful information leaflets and publications on many legal aspects of family separation.
Address: 64 Dame Street, Dublin 2
Tel.: (01) 6708363
E-mail: aimfamilyservices@eircom.net

AL-ANON-IRELAND
(http://www.al-anon-ireland.org)
Offers support for families of problem drinkers. The parents, children, wives, husbands and friends of alcoholics can be helped by Al-Anon. Alateen is for young people aged 12–17 who are affected by a problem drinker.
Address: Information Centre, Room 5, 5 Caple Street, Dublin 1
Tel.: (01) 8732699
E-mail: info@al-anon-ireland.org

AWARE
(http://www.aware.ie)
The Aware Helpline offers a confidential listening service for people affected by depression, either as sufferers or as family and friends. The helpline is also available to callers who are worried about someone who may be depressed or who wish to get information about depression or Aware services.
Address: 72 Lower Leeson Street, Dublin 2
Lo-call helpline: 1890 303 302
E-mail: info@aware.ie

BARNARDOS
(http://www.barnardos.ie)
Barnardos supports children whose well-being is under threat by working with them, their families and communities. Barnardos is one of Ireland's leading independent children's charities.
Address: National Children's Resource Centre, Christchurch Square, Dublin 8.
Tel.: (01) 454 9699
E-mail: ncrc@barnardos.ie

BODYWHYS
(http://www.bodywhys.ie)
BodyWhys offers support, information and understanding for people with eating disorders and support for their families and friends. It produces leaflets on all aspects of eating distress.

BodyWhysConnect is an online weekly support group that is available to people with an eating disorder over sixteen years of age.
Address: PO Box 105, Blackrock, Co. Dublin
Lo-call helpline: 1890 200 444
Tel.: (01) 283 4963
E-mail: alex@bodywhys.ie

CARI
(http://www.cari.ie)
CARI provides a confidential helpline service for anyone with concerns, feelings or fears regarding child sexual abuse. The helpline can also be used to access other CARI services or receive information or advice, or just to find someone to talk to.
Address: 110 Lower Drumcondra Road, Dublin 9
Lo-call helpline: 1890 9245 67
E-mail: helpline@cari.ie

CHILDLINE ONLINE
(http://www.childline.ie)
Childline provides a confidential listening service for all children and young people up to 18 years of age.

Childline Online will answer messages posted on the Childline message board for all young people. The website also provides information on specific topics such as bullying, family break-up and lots more.

Freephone helpline: 1800 666 666
Text Support (an automated service that provides a free text support service on a variety of issues): Text 'List' to 50101

CHILDREN'S RIGHTS ALLIANCE
(http://www.childrensrights.ie)
All children and young people up to the age of 18 years have rights under the UN Convention on the Rights of the Child. This website provides up-to-date information on developments affecting children and young people in Ireland.
Address: Children's Rights alliance, 4 Upper Mount Street, Dublin 2
Tel: (01) 662 9400
E-mail: info@childrensrights.ie

ASSOCIATION OF COLLABORATIVE PRACTITIONERS
(http://www.acp.ie)
Collaborative law is an alternative method of resolution of family disputes which helps separating couples (with the help of their collaborative lawyers) to resolve disputes and reach agreements on all issues arising without the need to go to court (except to legalise their agreement).
E-mail: info@acp.ie

DÁIL NA NÓG
(http://www.dailnanog.ie)
Dáil na nÓg means 'Youth Parliament' and gives an opportunity for young people in Ireland to have their views represented at a national level.
Address: National Youth Council of Ireland, 3 Montague Street, Dublin 2
Tel: (01) 478 4122
E-mail: info@dailnanog.ie

THE DRUGS AND ALCOHOL PROGRAMME (DAP)
(http://www.dap.ie)
DAP offers a wide range of services, including information, support and counselling in the area of drugs and alcohol. The site has a youth section – check it out. There is an interactive online live helper who will help answer your questions.
Address: Drugs Awareness Programme, Crosscare, The Red House, Clonliffe College, Dublin 3
Tel.: (01) 836 0911
E-mail: info@drugawareness.ie

THE FAMILY SUPPORT AGENCY
(http://www.fsa.ie)
The Family Support Agency provides a free service for couples, married and non-married, who have decided to separate or divorce and who want to negotiate together on the terms of their separation. Issues including living arrangements, parenting arrangements and financial issues are worked out together.
Address: St Stephen's Green House, Earlsfort Terrace, Dublin 2
Tel.: (01) 611 4100
E-mail: familsupportagency@welfare.ie

FREE LEGAL ADVICE CENTRES (FLAC)
(http://www.flac.ie)
FLAC provides an information and referral telephone line where you can call to get legal information and find details of your nearest centre where advice is also available.
Address: Free Legal Advice Centres, 13 Lower Dorset Street, Dublin 1
Lo-call helpline: 1890 350 250
Tel.: (01) 874 5690

GUARDIAN AD LITEM
(see the Barnardos website: http://www.barnardos.ie)

The Guardian ad Litem service provides children involved in family law proceedings with an independent voice in court. A Guardian ad Litem is an experienced and qualified person who is appointed by the court and advises on what is in the best interests of the child concerned, and makes the judge aware of the child's own wishes.

Address: Barnardos, National Children's Resource Centre, Christchurch Square, Dublin 8

Tel.: (01) 453 0355

E-mail: guardian@barnardos.ie

HEADSTRONG – NATIONAL CENTRE FOR YOUTH MENTAL HEALTH
(http://www.headstrong.ie)

Headstrong works with communities in Ireland to ensure that young people aged 12–25 are better supported to achieve mental health and well-being.

Address: 36 Waterloo Road, Ballsbridge, Dublin 4

E-mail: info@headstrong.ie

IRISH GUARDIAN AD LITEM SERVICES
(http://www.guardianadlitem.ie)

Irish Guardian ad Litem Services provides a comprehensive nationwide Guardian Ad Litem service to the Irish District Courts in all child care proceedings, as well as in the High Court Judicial Review proceedings.

E-mail: guardianadlitem@eircom.net

MARRIAGE AND RELATIONSHIP COUNSELLING SERVICES (MRCS)
(http://www.mrcs.ie)
MRCS is Ireland's longest established counselling agency for couples. It provides a non-denominational counselling service to people who are married or living together, single or separated, and who are experiencing difficulties in their marriage or relationship.
Address: 38 Upper Fitzwilliam Street, Dublin 2
Lo-call helpline: 1890 380 380
E-mail: info@mrcs.ie

NATIONAL YOUTH COUNCIL OF IRELAND (NYCI)
(http://www.youth.ie)
NYCI is a representative body for voluntary national youth organisations.
Address: 3 Montague Street, Dublin 2
Tel.: (01) 478 4122
E-mail: info@nyci.ie

OFFICE OF MINISTER OF CHILDREN
(www.omc.gov.ie)
The OMCYA is involved in policy issues that affect children in areas like early childhood care and education, youth justice, child welfare and protection, children and young people's participation, research on children and young people, and cross-cutting initiatives for children.
Address: Hawkins House, Dublin 2
Tel: (01) 635 4000
E-mail: omc@health.gov.ie

OMBUDSMAN FOR CHILDREN'S OFFICE (OCO)
(http://www.oco.ie)
The OCO helps ensure that the government and other people who make decisions about young people really think about what is best for them. This site contains a link to details of the UN Convention on the Rights of the Child.
E-mail: oco@oco.ie

ONE FAMILY
(http://www.onefamily.ie)
One Family is a leading national organisation for one-parent families, in Ireland. Provides services and support for one-parent families including training, education and a lo-call helpline.
Address: Cherish House, 2 Lower Pembroke Street, Dublin 2
Lo-call helpline: 1890 662 212
Tel.: (01) 662 9212
E-mail: info@onefamily.ie

PARENTLINE
(http://www.parentline.ie)
Parentline is a confidential helpline for parents under stress or who are worried about any aspect of parenting.
Lo-call Helpline: 1890 927 277
E-mail: info@parentline.ie

PRISONERS' FAMILY INFOLINE
This is a confidential service for anyone who is affected by the imprisonment of a family member, partner or friend.
Lo-call helpline: 1890 252578

RAINBOWS
(http://www.rainbowsireland.com)
Rainbows is a voluntary organisation that runs programmes for children, youth and adults who have experienced separation, divorce or other painful changes in their families. The Spectrum Programme is specifically made to support 12–18 year olds.
Address: Rainbows Ireland, Loreto Centre, Crumlin Road, Dublin 12
Tel.: (01) 473 4175
E-mail: ask@rainbowsireland.com

REHAB'S HEADSUP SERVICE
Headsup is the text support and information service provided by Rehab. It is a 24-hour texting service. Text the keyword 'Headsup' to the number 50424. A list of topics will be sent to you. Choose a topic and you will instantly be sent a list of confidential anonymous helpline numbers.

SAMARITANS
(http://www.samaritans.org)
Samaritans provides confidential support, 24 hours a day, for people who are experiencing feelings of distress or despair. The service is for anyone who is worried about something, feels upset or confused, or just wants to talk to someone. There are over 20 local branches of Samaritans in Ireland.
Tel.: 1850 60 90 90
E-mail: jo@samaritans.org

SCHIZOPHRENIA IRELAND
(http://www.sirl.ie)
Schizophrenia Ireland provides a range of information, support and services for those suffering from mental illness and, in particular, for family members who are caring and living with someone suffering from schizophrenia.
Address: 38 Blessington Street, Dublin 7
Tel.: 1890 621 631
E-mail: info@sirl.ie

SPUNOUT
(http://www.SpunOut.ie)
SpunOut, Ireland's National Youth Website, provides young people with an accessible, youth-led support service that is available all year round. It features many fact-sheets and articles covering issues such as bullying, exams, mental health, and many more.

TEEN BETWEEN®
(http://www.teenbetween.ie)
Teen Between is a specialised counselling service geared to helping 12–18 year olds cope with their parents' separation or divorce. Teen Between provides training to Youth Work Ireland and the Irish Guidance Counsellors' Association.
Address: 38 Upper Fitzwilliam Street, Dublin 2.
Tel.: (01) 678 5256
E-mail: teenbetween@mrcs.ie

TEEN COUNSELLING
(http://www.teencounselling.ie)
Teen Counselling is one of 12 programmes and services provided through Crosscare. Teen Counselling provides a professional counselling service for 12–18 year olds and their parents in relation to a wide range of issues and problems experienced by young people.
Address: Mater Dei, Clonliffe Road, Dublin 3
Tel.: (01) 837 1892
E-mail: materdei@teencounselling.com

TEENGROWTH
(http://www.teengrowth.com)
Teengrowth is an interactive website covering the general health interests and well-being of teenagers. It offers a secure site to search for, request and receive valuable health care information on topics such as alcohol, drugs, emotions, health, family, friends, school, sex and sports.

TEEN-LINE IRELAND
(http://www.teenline.ie)
Teen-line Ireland is a confidential helpline service set up to listen to teenagers about any problems or worries they may be having.
Freephone helpline: 1800 833 634
E-mail: info@teenline.ie

TEENSPACE
(http://www.teenspace.ie)
Teenspace is a website that provides information on events, activities and different recreation services aimed at young people aged 10–18 years. It is a national website giving information on all parts of the country and is

organised by Dáil na nÓg and the Office of the Minister for Children.
E-mail: editor@teenspace.ie

TREOIR
(http://www.treoir.ie)
Treoir is an organisation that provides free, confidential services and information for unmarried parents and their children. It operates a national information centre and has produced a useful leaflet on guardianship, access and custody of children whose parents are not married to each other.
Address: Gandon House, Custom House Square, IFSC, Dublin 1
Tel.: (01) 6700 120
Lo-call helpline: 1890 252 084
E-mail: info@treoir.ie

UNLOCKED
(http://www.unlocked.ie)
This site is great for news and information on anything alcohol related. It is not a site that lectures, but aims to better inform people so that it will be easier for them to make good choices and decisions for themselves regarding alcohol.